Fractured Identities

*For all of those who survived & succumbed.
To Remembrance, Reckoning, & Resilience.*

Fractured Identities: The Psychological Mechanisms of Sexual Violence During the 1947 Partition of India

Copyright © Krishna A. Patel 2025
All rights reserved

New York, NY

First Edition

ISBN-13: 979-8-9931733-0-6

LCCN is available at the Library of Congress.

An earlier version of this work was originally submitted as a graduate research project at Columbia University, South Asia Institute, May 2025.

Maps reproduced from public domain sources and archival material.

This is a work of scholarship. While every effort has been made to ensure the accuracy of information, the author and publisher assume no responsibility for errors or omissions.

Cover and interior design by the author.

Printed in the United States of America

COLUMBIA UNIVERSITY
SOUTH ASIA INSTITUTE

FRACTURED IDENTITIES:

THE PSYCHOLOGICAL MECHANISMS OF SEXUAL VIOLENCE
DURING THE 1947 PARTITION OF INDIA

KRISHNA A. PATEL

This page left intentionally blank

Columbia University
Graduate School of Arts & Sciences
South Asia Institute

FRACTURED IDENTITIES:
The Psychological Mechanisms of Sexual
Violence During the 1947 Partition of India

KRISHNA A. PATEL

Originally Submitted
May 2025

ACKNOWLEDGMENTS

This book is not solely the product of my individual efforts; it is the culmination of the guidance, support, and belief of an extraordinary community to whom I owe a profound debt of gratitude.

First, I extend my deepest thanks to Columbia University and the South Asia Institute (SAI) for providing a scholarly home where difficult questions could be asked and transformative learning could flourish. Columbia has given me not just an education but a space to reckon with history, memory, and moral responsibility.

To Dr. Valerie Purdie-Greenaway, my advisor and mentor, I offer my boundless appreciation. Your wisdom, rigor, and compassion carried me through every stage of this process. You taught me not only how to build arguments, but how to honor truth—and that is a lesson I will carry with me far beyond these pages.

I am also grateful to Dr. Syantani Chatterjee, Director of the SAI MA program, whose vision and commitment shaped this journey in immeasurable ways, and to Mr. William Carrick, Associate Director of SAI, whose constant encouragement and support were vital during moments of doubt.

To my family—my parents, Arvind and Rupali, who sacrificed and dreamed so that I could reach this place; my sister and brother-in-law, Arti and Saajan, who constantly believed in me; my grandmother, Pushpa, whose resilience continues to inspire me; and my loyal dogs, Blaze and Milo, who gave me unconditional love when I needed it the most—you are the foundation upon which everything stands. Every word in this book is built upon your love.

I am blessed to be surrounded by friends who are family: Vidisha, Karthick, Anjali, Neda, Sehyr, and Ashley—thank you for your faith, your laughter, and your unwavering presence when I needed it most.

To my forever advocate and grounder, Chelsea, thank you for your guidance, trust, and boundless support as I navigated this heavy undertaking. You taught me to believe in myself when I needed it the most.

To my former co-workers, Krista and Jan, thank you for pushing me to dream bigger, for seeing potential in me when I doubted myself, and for encouraging me to pursue this life-changing opportunity at Columbia.

Most importantly, I dedicate this work to the survivors of the Partition of India, to those who were lost to its unspeakable violence, and to the region itself—a land of fractured identities and enduring hope. Their courage, their silences, and their memories shaped the moral center of this book. It is their voices, above all, that I seek to honor.

Finally, but never least, I thank God—especially Amba Maa, Santoshi Maa, and Kaali Maa—for guiding me through this emotionally wrenching research. In the darkest moments, when history weighed heavily and words faltered, their grace gave me the strength to continue.

This study is dedicated to remembrance, to reckoning, and to resilience.

Learn from history. Set forth to grow from it. Most importantly, guide a better future than the one left behind.

TABLE OF CONTENTS

Acknowledgments 9

Abstract 17

Maps of India Pre-Partition................19

Introduction 23
Research Questions and Hypothesis

Methodology

Key Terms

Justifying the Method and Addressing Counterarguments

Partition Scholarship & Ethics

Chapter 1: Theoretical Framework – Moral Disengagement, Opportunity, and Group Violence..59
Moral Disengagement

Dehumanization

Group Obedience and Peer Pressure

Situational Enablers

Gendered Violence in Ethnic Conflicts

Synthesis: Interlocking Mechanisms of Violence

Looking Forward: Regional Application of the Framework

Chapter 2: Historical Context – Sexual Violence in the Partition Across Regions 95
> ***Punjab***: *The Epicenter of Partition Violence*
>
> ***Bengal***: *Urban Centers and the Role of Political Rhetoric*
>
> ***Sindh***: *Forced Conversions and Political Opportunism*
>
> ***Kashmir***: *Territorial Conflict and the Gendered Battlefield*
>
> *Case Study Synthesis*

Chapter 3: Perpetrator Justifications and Moral Disengagement 147

Chapter 4: Psychological & Situational Mechanisms in Action…............................177

The Role of Peer Pressure and Collective Identity Formation

Ritualization of Sexual Violence and Symbolic Communication

Comparative Perspectives and Reinforcing the Thesis

Addressing Counterarguments

Chapter 5: Conclusion – Implications for Partition and Genocide Studies................213

Glossary of Terms 239

References 245

ABSTRACT

The 1947 Partition of India remains one of the bloodiest and most transformative events of the twentieth century, marked not only by mass displacement and communal violence but also by widespread sexual atrocities that have long been marginalized in historical discourse. This study examines how moral disengagement functioned as a psychological mechanism enabling mass sexual violence during the Partition, arguing that such disengagement was neither accidental nor chaotic but systematically conditioned through social, emotional, and institutional structures. Drawing upon Albert Bandura's moral disengagement theory, supported by interdisciplinary insights from genocide studies, criminology, and survivor testimony, this study applies a qualitative thematic analysis to survivor narratives, governmental documents, and media discourses. It reveals how perpetrators justified acts of brutality through mechanisms such as dehumanization, euphemistic labeling, group conformity, and emotional catalysts like fear and revenge, all amplified by the situational collapse of law and order.

Through regional case studies across Punjab, Bengal, Sindh, and Kashmir, the study demonstrates that despite differing local dynamics, the cognitive architecture of violence remained consistent. Perpetrators were not aberrations but ordinary individuals who rationalized cruelty as communal duty or spiritual redemption. In doing so, this study challenges simplistic explanations of Partition violence as mere chaos, revealing instead a complex interplay between psychological processes and historical contingencies. It further argues that the silence surrounding sexual violence during the Partition has perpetuated collective moral disengagement, allowing narratives of honor, sacrifice, and national pride to overwrite survivors' experiences. By confronting these silences and mapping the architecture of moral disengagement, this study offers critical insights not only into the Partition but into the enduring patterns of mass violence globally—making it an essential reading for historians, psychologists, policymakers, and advocates of transitional justice.

Fractured Identities | 19

Maps of India Pre-1947 Partition

Political divisions of the Indian Empire, 1909. Reprinted from *Atlas, Plate 20, Imperial Gazetteer of India*, by Clarendon Press, 1909.

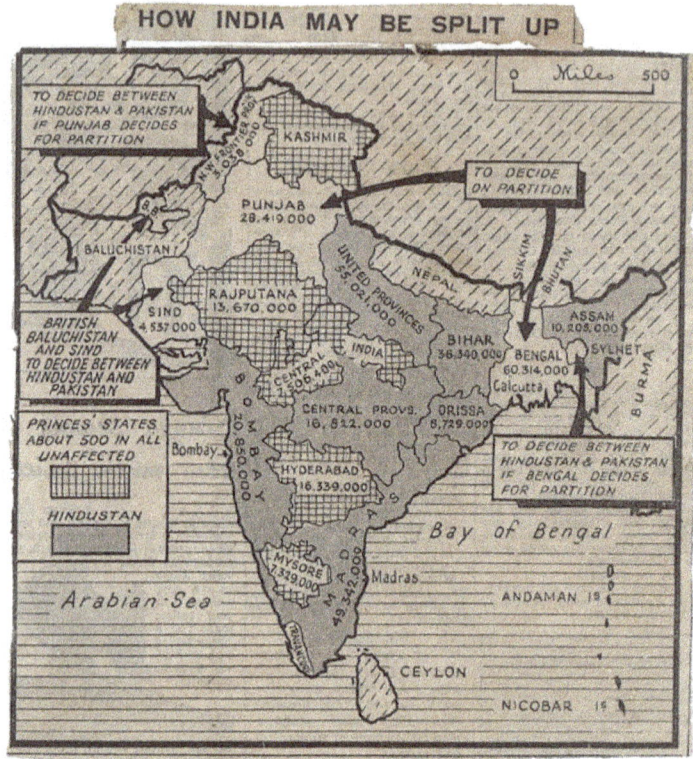

How India may be split up, 1947. Reprinted from *Daily Mail* (London), March 4, 1947. Public domain

This page left intentionally blank

INTRODUCTION

The Partition of India in 1947 remains one of the most violent and transformative events of the twentieth century, marked by unprecedented displacement, communal hostility, and a level of brutality that has continued to shape South Asian memory and politics. Among its most disturbing legacies is the mass sexual violence that accompanied the upheaval—rape, abduction, forced conversion, and public humiliation, which became tools of communal retribution and domination. Despite the centrality of this violence to the Partition's historical record, its psychological and sociocultural underpinnings remain underexplored. This study seeks to address that gap by examining how moral disengagement functioned as a psychological mechanism enabling mass sexual violence during the Partition, arguing that such disengagement was not merely a product of wartime chaos but a systematically conditioned cognitive and social process. This study is not simply about recovering the past—it is about understanding the patterns that allowed such violence to unfold and continue unchallenged. Sexual violence during the Partition was not an incidental product of chaos, but a core method of asserting communal power, symbolizing domination, and morally justifying cruelty. To ignore its structure is to overlook one of the most critical elements of mass violence: the way violence is psychologically and culturally rationalized before, during, and after it is committed. This makes the Partition a case study not only in failed governance and geopolitical mismanagement but in the failure of communities to resist the slide into moral collapse.

Psychology is a vital, though often overlooked, tool for understanding and preventing mass violence. While political scientists and historians can map the external factors—borders drawn, armies mobilized, governments collapsed—it is psychology that asks how ordinary people become complicit in extraordinary harm. Bandura's theory of moral disengagement offers a profound lens into this question, helping to see how social narratives, emotional catalysts, and institutional failures interact to suspend ethical judgment. This book demonstrates that understanding perpetrators' internal justifications is not a distraction from justice but a necessary precondition to its achievement. By understanding how violence is made thinkable, it assists in ways to unthink it—through education, accountability, and truth-telling.

Examining the Partition of India through this lens also helps correct the historical imbalance that has long ignored or minimized the role of sexual violence. Despite the scale of abuse, public discourse in both India and Pakistan continues to treat sexual violence as an uncomfortable footnote rather than a defining feature of the Partition's brutality. The erasure has profound implications—not only for survivors and their descendants but for how society comes to understand violence, justice, and national identity. By restoring the prominence of sexual violence in Partition scholarship, this study insists on telling fuller, more honest histories—ones that do not excuse atrocity for the sake of patriotism.

Additionally, the Partition remains a deeply relevant topic in South Asia today, not just for historical reasons but for its resonance in current communal tensions and gendered violence. In contemporary India and Pakistan, majoritarianism, religious polarization, and political rhetoric continue to echo many of the justifications for violence heard in 1947. This makes the Partition an object of study and a living context—a mirror held up to the present. If the operationalization of moral disengagement can be traced, then it may help to better understand how to interrupt it now. This book serves as both a diagnosis and a warning: the psychological scripts of atrocity remain active, and without intervention, they will write new chapters.

The themes of this book resonate far beyond the historical moment of the Partition. In the rising tide of communalism, nationalism, and mass disinformation across the globe, understanding how violence is made thinkable is more urgent than ever. The case of the Partition offers a cautionary tale and a diagnostic lens—a way to identify the social and psychological signs of moral collapse before atrocity becomes normalized. While no two conflicts are identical, the cognitive mechanisms that enable cruelty have appeared time and again in different corners of the world, echoing in the voices of perpetrators who say, "We had no choice," or "We were defending our community." These echoes reveal the dangerous elasticity of moral judgment in moments of crisis.

One of the most enduring contributions of this study is the integration of survivor voices alongside the theories used to explain perpetrator behavior. This approach is not only methodologically rigorous but ethically necessary. The survivors of the Partition are not just subjects in a historical tragedy—they are the stewards of moral truth, bearing witness to acts that society has tried to forget. By centering their words, their pain, and their insights, this book challenges the sanitized historical record and insists that understanding violence requires listening closely to those who endured it. Their accounts, full of both horror and resilience, deepen the understanding of the psychological, cultural, and institutional dimensions of sexual violence.

The findings of this study also suggest that prevention efforts must move upstream—toward the moments when moral disengagement begins, not just when it is fully formed. Educational curricula that examine how language, ideology, and silence operate as mechanisms of moral transformation could provide a crucial safeguard against future atrocities. Similarly, legal and transitional justice frameworks must move beyond punitive measures to address the social conditions that allow violence to be reframed as virtue. Truth commissions, memory projects, and public rituals of accountability all have roles to play, but only if they confront the psychological legacies of past violence and offer apparent moral alternatives.

This study ultimately serves as a call to responsibility. It invites readers—scholars, policymakers, educators, and community members—to interrogate the moral scaffolding of their societies. It demands that the examination is not just into who committed violence, but how entire communities enabled it, justified it, and moved on from it without repair. In posing these questions, this book contributes not just to the study of the Partition, but to a larger reckoning with the moral architecture of violence. It is an invitation to remember, to reckon, and to resist.

Research Questions and Hypothesis

The central research question guiding this study is:

How did moral disengagement and its accompanying psychological mechanisms—such as dehumanization, diffusion of responsibility, and emotional catalysts—converge with situational enablers to permit widespread sexual violence during the 1947 Partition of India?

Subsidiary Questions:

- What psychological and communal rationalizations did perpetrators use to justify acts of sexual violence?
- How did regional and environmental differences influence the expression of these rationalizations?
- What role did political rhetoric, institutional silence, and media narratives play in reinforcing moral disengagement?

Hypothesis: Moral disengagement was a necessary but insufficient psychological mechanism that enabled mass sexual violence during the 1947 Partition of India. While it provided perpetrators with cognitive justification, the actual commission of violence was catalyzed by a convergence of situational enablers (lawlessness, mob dynamics), social pressures (peer conformity, community approval), and emotional triggers (communal rage, fear, grief). These conditions created a moral vacuum in which sexual violence was not only permissible but reframed as righteous, necessary, or even heroic.

The core research question guiding this study is: How did moral disengagement and its accompanying psychological mechanisms—such as dehumanization, diffusion of responsibility, and emotional catalysts—converge with situational enablers to permit widespread sexual violence during the 1947 Partition of India? In approaching this question, the study adopts a multidisciplinary framework, drawing from social psychology, genocide studies, and historical testimony. It applies Albert Bandura's moral disengagement theory to explain how individuals justified extreme acts of violence, particularly against women, and how these justifications were reinforced by group conformity, emotional provocation, and the breakdown of institutional authority.

Methodology

The methodology of this study uses qualitative thematic analysis of survivor testimonies, oral histories, government records, and contemporary newspapers with interpretive applications of social theory. Primary sources include The 1947 Partition Archive, *The Other Side of Silence* by Urvashi Butalia, and *Borders & Boundaries* by Ritu Menon and Kamla Bhasin. The study also draws from public media reports published in *The Statesman* and *Dawn* during the Partition period, alongside official documentation such as The Abducted Persons (Recovery and Restoration) Act of 1949. These sources are analyzed for recurring justifications, euphemistic language, and evidence of group-based rationalization.

This study is significant not only because it sheds light on a neglected aspect of the Partition, but because it contributes to broader efforts to understand how mass atrocities—especially gendered violence—are made morally permissible by ordinary individuals. The study contends that sexual violence during the Partition was not merely an outcome of disorder, but the result of deeply embedded moral narratives that reframed cruelty as virtue. By focusing on the psychology of perpetrators rather than solely on structural or ideological explanations, this study opens new pathways for both historical accountability and future prevention.

The structure of the book is as follows: Chapter 1 presents the theoretical framework, detailing the psychological theories that inform the analysis. Chapter 2 applies this framework to regional case studies across Punjab, Bengal, Sindh, and Kashmir, illustrating how moral disengagement was locally adapted. Chapter 3 explores how perpetrators justified their actions and how silence, media, and social norms reinforced these justifications. Chapter 4 examines the behavioral translation of these rationalizations, addressing how emotional and situational factors catalyzed actual acts of sexual violence. Chapter 5 concludes the study by synthesizing the findings and exploring their implications for memory, justice, and prevention.

Key Terms:

Communal Violence: Organized or spontaneous violence between religious, ethnic, or communal groups, motivated by perceived historical grievances, territorial claims, or symbolic assertions of superiority, as exemplified during the 1947 Partition of India (Khan, 2007; Talbot & Singh, 2009).

Dehumanization: The psychological mechanism through which victims are stripped of their human qualities and viewed as subhuman or morally expendable (Smith, 2011).

Moral Disengagement: The process by which individuals justify or rationalize unethical behavior, thereby disengaging from their own internal moral standards (Bandura, 1999).

Perpetrators: Ordinary individuals, militia members, or community actors who actively engaged in acts of sexual violence, abduction, or symbolic humiliation during the Partition, often justified through communal narratives and moral disengagement (Waller, 2007; Browning, 1992).

Rape: The act of non-consensual sexual penetration, used systematically during Partition as a form of communal punishment, symbolic conquest, and erasure of identity. Often framed as retributive justice during Partition's communal violence (Menon & Bhasin, 1998; Das, 2007).

Ritualized Violence: Acts of violence that are symbolically structured and often repeated, serving to reinforce communal narratives and boundaries (Sharlach, 2000; Das, 2007).

Sexual Violence: Acts of a sexual nature perpetrated through coercion, force, or intimidation, used as tools of communal domination, humiliation, and ethnic cleansing during mass violence events such as Partition. (Menon & Bhasin, 1998; Sharlach, 2000)

Situational Enablers: Environmental or institutional factors that create the conditions for violence to occur, including lawlessness, mob dynamics, and state inaction (Cohen & Felson, 1979; Khan, 2007).

Survivors/Victims: Individuals, primarily women, who experienced sexual violence, abduction, forced conversion, and communal humiliation during Partition. Survivors' testimonies serve as critical sources for understanding the moral and psychological architecture of violence (Butalia, 1998; Das, 2007).

Violence: Physical, psychological, and symbolic harm inflicted intentionally on individuals or groups, often ritualized and normalized within communities to assert dominance or preserve group identity during Partition (Das, 2007; Smith, 2011).

Justifying the Method and Addressing Counterarguments

Some scholars may argue that applying psychological frameworks—especially those developed in Western contexts—to a postcolonial event like the Partition risks misrepresenting the cultural and historical specificities of South Asia. However, this study contends that the psychological processes it analyzes, particularly moral disengagement, are not culturally exclusive. Bandura's theory has been applied across genocidal and conflict scenarios from the Holocaust to Rwanda, and the mechanisms it outlines—justification, euphemism, dehumanization, diffusion of responsibility—are observable in both highly organized and decentralized violence. By anchoring these theories within culturally situated case studies across Punjab, Bengal, Sindh, and Kashmir, this study avoids universalizing trauma while still drawing on comparative analytical tools that reveal disturbing global consistencies in the moral logic of atrocities.

Additionally, some may contend that the study of perpetrator psychology risks sidelining the lived experiences of survivors or unintentionally humanizing those responsible for violence. This study takes that critique seriously and addresses it by positioning survivor testimonies at the heart of its analysis. The psychological mechanisms discussed are not abstract theories imposed on data; they are directly drawn from the language and patterns evident in oral histories and archival material. Far from minimizing survivor voices, this methodology illuminates how victims themselves understood and narrated the rationalizations used against them. As Veena Das suggests, examining the discourse of violence helps us understand how it becomes embedded in everyday life (Das, 2007, p. 64). By analyzing the perpetrator's mindset and the survivor's response, this book offers a more comprehensive account of how moral disengagement operates systemically.

Finally, this approach is particularly suited to the topic at hand because it accounts for the deeply symbolic and gendered nature of violence observed during the Partition. It allows exploring the cognitive processes of perpetrators and how those processes were enabled by their environment, reinforced by communal narratives, and validated by institutional inaction. Unlike more limited legalistic or statistical approaches, this method provides a layered, interdisciplinary lens that connects internal justification with external conditions. In this way, it ensures that this analysis not only incorporates what perpetrators did but also how they came to believe it was morally permissible. This dual insight is essential for building future models of violence prevention, historical understanding, and ethical accountability. In such settings, traditional legal or structural analyses alone are insufficient. They cannot fully explain why neighbors turned on neighbors, why violence was performed publicly, or why communities engaged in acts of ritualized humiliation. A psychological lens, especially one grounded in moral disengagement theory, provides the tools to understand how violence becomes communal, morally permissible, and emotionally sustainable. This method does not replace structural or historical explanations—it complements them, revealing how individual cognition intersects with broader ideological and institutional failures to produce acts of mass atrocity.

Partition Scholarship & Ethics

Ultimately, this book is both a scholarly and ethical undertaking. It seeks not only to explain how the Partition's sexual violence occurred, but to challenge the moral frameworks that allowed it to happen—and that still permit its erasure. In doing so, it calls for a deeper reckoning with how communities narrate violence, how perpetrators come to see themselves as righteous, and how society might break these cycles through truth, memory, and moral clarity. It builds upon an understanding that violence is not simply a matter of physical acts but a reflection of how communities construct moral hierarchies and define belonging. This study argues that mass sexual violence cannot be relegated to the shadows of historical aberration—it must be treated as a central, intentional outcome of cognitive and cultural processes that made such acts conceivable, permissible, and often celebrated. By shifting the focus from what happened to how and why it was permitted, scholars gain the conceptual tools to diagnose and confront the recurrence of such violence today and to establish a methodological roadmap for future interdisciplinary analysis of mass violence. Through its combination of social psychology, historical analysis, and survivor-centered testimony, this study sets a standard for how complex trauma and communal violence can be studied without reducing them to oversimplified narratives. This holistic methodology invites future scholars to explore violence not just in terms of actors and victims, but as a system of beliefs, narratives, and institutional breakdowns that coalesce under conditions of crisis. It also models a way to write history with ethical clarity, refusing the dispassionate detachment that often characterizes scholarship on atrocity. Instead, this work insists that emotion, empathy, and critical engagement must coexist if society is to understand the human cost of violence truly.

The interdisciplinary rigor of this study does not dilute its focus—it sharpens it. By reading political archives alongside psychological texts, and survivor testimonies alongside perpetrator justifications, the research reveals connections that a single-disciplinary approach might overlook. It makes clear that sexual violence during the Partition was not an anomaly, but a coherent outcome of ideological narratives that made cruelty intelligible. Such a framework encourages asking difficult questions about the moral economies of violence: who is allowed to suffer, who is permitted to act, and how those actions are made narratively acceptable within communities. These are questions that resonate far beyond South Asia, challenging societies everywhere to consider how the seeds of violence are planted in language, belief, and silence.

Additionally, this study also affirms that academic scholarship can be a form of activism. In uncovering suppressed stories, exposing the structures that enabled them, and situating them within broader global patterns of atrocity, the work challenges dominant narratives and creates space for counter-memory. It argues that academic work is not neutral—it is either complicit in silencing or active in disrupting silence. By choosing the latter path, this book aligns itself with survivors, with memory, and with the call for justice that echoes across time and borderlines. In this way, the book becomes more than a study—it becomes a refusal to forget.

In acknowledging the survivors who offered their stories—whether through formal interviews or written testimonies—this study seeks to return dignity to those who were stripped of it by both violence and the historical record. It affirms that survivors are not just subjects of inquiry but holders of essential knowledge, capable of challenging entrenched myths and reshaping collective memory. Their testimonies do more than describe violence—they expose its logic, its routinization, and its devastating aftermath. To center these voices is not only an ethical imperative but a methodological strength, allowing for a narrative that is both analytical and accountable.

As violence continues to resurface globally in the form of ethnic cleansing, gendered repression, and authoritarian resurgence, the lessons of this study remain urgent. Understanding how ordinary people become perpetrators, how communities endorse atrocity, and how silence becomes complicity is essential for any society aspiring for justice. The Partition may have taken place over seventy-five years ago, but the moral questions it raises remain alive in headlines, policy debates, and cultural reckonings around the world. This book contributes to those debates not just by looking back, but by offering frameworks for vigilance today.

Even within academia, the topic of the Partition remains fragmented, often isolated within national, disciplinary, or ideological silos. This study attempts to bridge those divides by insisting that the Partition cannot be studied as a standalone event—it must be understood as part of a transnational history of displacement, sexual violence, and moral reckoning. In doing so, it provides a template for future comparative work that links South Asia to other regions marked by communal rupture and trauma. It invites scholars to move beyond bounded categories and instead pursue a shared inquiry into how violence is justified, enacted, and remembered.

The comprehensive analysis of the Partition through these theoretical frameworks is a testament to the necessity of truth in scholarship. It refuses the erasures that have long haunted the study of the Partition and insists on naming what was done, how it was justified, and why it must be remembered. It is a work of mourning and a call to action. For the survivors who endured, for the histories yet to be written, and for the futures in need of protection, this book stands as both a reckoning and a beginning.

The psychological lens used throughout this study is especially powerful because it offers a way to move beyond binary moral judgments and toward a deeper understanding of complicity. It reveals that perpetrators are often not sadistic outliers but rather ordinary individuals who come to see their violence as necessary or even virtuous. This insight compels us to confront the everyday nature of moral disengagement—the way it permeates public discourse, cultural norms, and institutional behavior. In exploring these pathways, this study also provides a vocabulary for resistance: terms such as euphemistic labeling, dehumanization, and displacement of responsibility become diagnostic tools for understanding when societies are at risk of justifying atrocities.

Furthermore, the interdisciplinary approach of this study sets a precedent for future scholarship on violence and memory. By weaving together psychological theory, historical documentation, survivor testimony, and regional analysis, the study examines past atrocities and models a method for ethically engaged research. It demonstrates the value of combining empirical rigor with moral urgency—a synthesis that is essential when the stakes involve both justice for victims and the prevention of future violence. This approach can and should be adapted to other sites of trauma, offering scholars a template for investigating the moral architecture of violence across contexts.

A key goal of this book is also to challenge the dominant frameworks that tend to compartmentalize violence—dividing it into political, communal, or gender-based categories. Such divisions, while analytically useful at times, risk obscuring the interconnectedness of how violence functions. Sexual violence during the Partition, for example, was simultaneously communal and gendered, symbolic and tactical, spontaneous and systematized. Recognizing this complexity not only enriches historical understanding but expands ethical responsibility. South Asian and Genocide scholarship must move beyond siloed interpretations and, instead, acknowledge violence as a multidimensional process shaped by overlapping systems of power and belief.

The findings also encourage a reexamination of national narratives that seek to build cohesion through omission. In both India and Pakistan, the story of the Partition is often told in ways that glorify sacrifice, resilience, and religious triumph. But these narratives omit the thousands of women who were raped, abducted, and forced into silence, treating them as collateral damage rather than as central figures in the national story. This erasure is not neutral—it is, in itself, a form of moral disengagement. This book challenges such erasure by insisting that these women's experiences are not peripheral but fundamental to any honest reckoning with the Partition.

In examining these silences, the study also contributes to the field of memory studies. It shows how collective memory is not simply what is remembered but what is sanctioned, repeated, and institutionalized. The stories that are told, and those that are buried, reveal the moral priorities of a society. By analyzing how the Partition's sexual violence has been remembered—or forgotten—this book highlights the relationship between narrative, identity, and justice. It asserts that memory is a battleground and that reclaiming suppressed stories is a form of resistance.

Ultimately, this book aims to make visible what has been systematically hidden—not only in the historical archive but in the moral imagination of the nation. It seeks to restore agency and voice to survivors while exposing the ideological and psychological scaffolding that allowed violence to thrive. In doing so, it reclaims not just history but ethics, arguing that how society remembers the past is inseparable from how it builds a more just and humane future. Additionally, it helps to underline the moral urgency of this undertaking. It is not simply an academic contribution but a framework for future inquiry, justice-oriented education, and historical repair. The Partition continues to live in silences—unspoken trauma, generational fear, and unresolved memory—and this book insists on disrupting that silence with scholarly rigor and ethical commitment. Through its detailed unpacking of psychological mechanisms and cultural narratives, it pushes for new models of recognition, responsibility, and reform. This work does not claim to offer closure, but it provides the vocabulary and vision to begin a different kind of conversation about violence—one rooted in empathy, precision, and truth.

CHAPTER 1

THEORETICAL FRAMEWORK – MORAL DISENGAGEMENT, OPPORTUNITY, AND GROUP VIOLENCE

This chapter lays the theoretical foundation for the study, exploring the psychological and criminological frameworks that help explain the perpetration of sexual violence during the 1947 Partition of India into two states: India and Pakistan. It draws upon the interdisciplinary work of scholars Albert Bandura, David Livingstone Smith, James Waller, Stanley Milgram, Christopher Browning, and others to build a conceptual understanding of how ordinary individuals became capable of committing acts of mass sexual violence. The argument is that the theory of moral disengagement enabled perpetrators to rationalize their actions, while group conformity, situational enablers, and emotional catalysts triggered actual violent behaviors.

To understand how these psychological mechanisms operate in contexts of extreme political violence, it is essential to consider how rapidly shifting social landscapes can influence moral cognition. The 1947 Partition created an unprecedented rupture in the subcontinent's social and political order. Mass displacement, the sudden dissolution of colonial authority, and the vacuum left by British withdrawal disrupted everyday life and intensified communal hostilities. In this environment, acts of violence previously unthinkable to most became normalized, and the moral codes that typically constrain behavior were easily suspended or inverted. It is within this social upheaval that psychological mechanisms such as moral disengagement found fertile ground.

Moreover, the communal dimension of Partition violence intensified these psychological processes. Unlike violence in conventional warfare, where distinctions between combatants and civilians are often more apparent, Partition-era violence blurred these boundaries as communal tensions launched various communities into committing acts of violence against one another. Neighbors turned on neighbors, and the perception of religious or communal identity superseded all other affiliations. As David Livingstone Smith notes, dehumanization is most potent when social divisions are marked and deeply internalized (Smith, 2011). During the Partition, identity became weaponized, and sexual violence was not merely interpersonal but symbolic—aimed at desecrating the body of the enemy collective through individual harm.

Moral Disengagement (Bandura, 1999)

Albert Bandura's theory of moral disengagement is central to this study. In *Moral Disengagement: How People Do Harm and Live with Themselves (1999)*, Bandura defines the process of moral disengagement as one in which individuals disengage their internal moral standards to participate in actions that would normally cause guilt or cognitive dissonance (Bandura, 1999).

Bandura's framework is particularly useful for examining collective violence that is spontaneous and decentralized, such as what occurred during the Partition. Unlike state-sponsored genocides where orders are issued from above, Partition violence was often executed by everyday people—neighbors, villagers, and passersby—who acted with an internal sense of justification. Bandura emphasizes that moral disengagement can occur in localized contexts where individuals draw upon cultural, religious, or political ideologies to distance themselves from the harm they inflict. In the Indian subcontinent, longstanding communal narratives about honor, pollution, and retaliation gave moral weight to actions that would otherwise be unthinkable.

One particularly salient feature of moral disengagement during the Partition was the invocation of collective suffering to justify retaliation. As scholars like Yasmin Khan have noted in *The Great Partition (2007)*, stories of "our women" being abducted or raped spread rapidly across newly drawn borders, creating a cyclical logic of revenge (Khan, 2007). This led perpetrators to view sexual violence not as an individual crime but as a symbolic act of communal restoration. In such cases, perpetrators often framed their actions as protective or reparative, even when the acts themselves were deeply violent and dehumanizing. This illustrates Bandura's notion of "moral justification" taken to its most extreme conclusion—where violence is seen not just as tolerable, but as righteous.

Moreover, Bandura discusses how displacement of responsibility can emerge through hierarchical or collective structures, such as mobs. During the Partition, many testimonies indicate that sexual violence occurred in group settings, where individual responsibility was diluted. In *Borders & Boundaries (1998)*, Menon and Bhasin document cases where attackers claimed they had no choice or were "just following" the actions of others in the group. This diffusion of responsibility allowed perpetrators to maintain a positive self-image, as they did not perceive themselves as the sole agents of harm. Such group dynamics were crucial in enabling ordinary individuals to become participants in acts of mass violence. This process involves several mechanisms:

Moral justification: Reframing harmful behavior as being in service of a higher moral purpose (e.g., religion, nationalism, honor).

Euphemistic labeling: Using sanitizing language to disguise the nature of the violence (e.g., referring to rape as "punishment" or "honor restoration").

Dehumanization: Stripping victims of human qualities, rendering them "other" or subhuman.

Displacement and diffusion of responsibility: Shifting accountability to others, often through group settings, where actions are carried out by mobs or in the name of the collective.

These mechanisms are not abstract concepts but appear frequently in testimonies from survivors of the Partition. In *The Other Side of Silence (1998)*, Urvashi Butalia records interviews where women describe being raped by men who claimed they were "restoring community honor." This aligns with the presented definitions of moral justification and euphemistic labeling (Bandra, 1999).

Dehumanization (David Livingstone Smith, 2011)

Smith's *Less Than Human (2011)* complements Bandura's theory by examining how dehumanization serves as a psychological precondition for violence. He claims that dehumanization makes it easier for perpetrators to commit atrocities because victims are no longer seen as human beings deserving of empathy or protection (Smith, 2011). During the Partition, survivors often recall being treated as "impure," "defiled," or "enemy property," reflecting this process. Ritu Menon and Kamla Bhasin's *Borders & Boundaries (1998)* further illustrate how the female body became a battlefield on which communal identities were fought and erased (Menon & Bhasin, 1998).

Smith's analysis is particularly relevant in cases where violence is not just meant to eliminate but to humiliate and erase. During the Partition, dehumanization operated on both symbolic and physical levels. The acts of stripping a victim of their clothing, forcing them to convert religions, or parading them through villages before rape were all tactics aimed at severing their identity from personhood. These actions reflect what

Smith terms as "mechanisms of exclusion," where victims are placed outside the moral community, allowing the perpetrator to view them not as human beings, but as representations of a threatening other (Smith, 2011).

Furthermore, the communal narrative around purity and honor intensified the dehumanization of the perceived enemy. In Hindu and Muslim communities alike, women were seen as bearers of communal honor. Violating a woman from the rival community symbolically defiled the collective group. Such logic relies on the abstraction of women into symbols, stripping them of personhood. In this way, rape became a language of violence through which communities communicated revenge, dominance, and existential triumph during the Partition.

Menon and Bhasin's documentation of women being forcibly tattooed with religious symbols, converted, or renamed demonstrates how Partition-era sexual violence operated as both a physical and symbolic assault. These were not isolated acts of cruelty, but calculated strategies enabled by a psychological framework that first stripped the victim of their humanity. The ability of individuals to carry out such acts without remorse points to the role of dehumanization as a necessary psychological step in the commission of extreme violence.

Dehumanization during the Partition took multiple forms: portraying women from other religious groups as dishonorable, associating them with pollution, or targeting them for forced conversion or rape to "cleanse" bloodlines. These acts required a breakdown of moral empathy, which Smith argues is facilitated through constructed narratives of otherness.

Group Obedience and Peer Pressure (Milgram, Browning)

The work of Stanley Milgram (*Obedience to Authority, 1974*) and Christopher Browning (*Ordinary Men, 1992*) provides insight into how social structures and authority figures influence ordinary people to commit violence. Milgram's experiments show that individuals will comply with harmful commands if they believe they are acting under legitimate authority. Browning, in his study of Reserve Police Battalion 101 during the Holocaust, argues that peer pressure and fear of social ostracization, rather than ideological commitment, were the primary motivators behind participation in mass killings. While the Holocaust was a state-designated genocide, these scholars put forth foundational work on groupthink that translated in the case of the Partition.

Milgram's findings are particularly illuminating because they demonstrate how the pressure to conform can override personal morality. In many of the testimonies from the 1947 Partition Archive, survivors recount that perpetrators acted in groups where no single individual seemed to take full responsibility. This echoes Milgram's conclusion that people are more likely to obey orders or follow the group when they perceive a diffusion of responsibility and an external authority figure—even if that authority is social rather than formal. In the chaos of the Partition, community leaders, religious figures, or dominant males often took on informal authority roles, setting the tone for violent action and making participation feel obligatory.

Browning's study of *Reserve Police Battalion 101* also underscores how violence becomes normalized through repeated exposure and the desire to belong. He found that many individuals committed atrocities not out of hatred but to avoid being ostracized or labeled as cowards by their peers (Browning, 1992). In the Partition, the same pattern emerges.

Oral histories describe men who participated in rapes or abductions not out of ideological fervor but because they feared the repercussions of non-participation in a tightly knit and increasingly radicalized group. This peer-driven coercion reveals how communal violence can escalate rapidly, driven more by interpersonal dynamics than by political ideology alone. Furthermore, this group-based dynamic contributed to the breakdown of individual ethical reflection. When acts of sexual violence became embedded in communal rituals of revenge or assertion of dominance, they lost their status as crimes in the minds of perpetrators. The social rewards of participation—honor, loyalty, communal belonging—came to outweigh the moral costs. Waller's *Becoming Evil (2002)* aptly summarizes this when he notes that group-based violence often functions by flipping moral norms, making acts of cruelty not just permissible but celebrated within the group's moral code.

Applying this to the Partition, we see similar dynamics: group violence often involved perpetrators acting in mobs, driven not by ideological extremism alone but also by social conformity. Survivors from Punjab and Bengal, in testimonies collected by the 1947 Partition Archive, recount that rapes and abductions were often carried out by large groups of men. Some survivors even report that perpetrators cited fear of looking weak or disloyal as justification for participating.

James Waller's *Becoming Evil (2002)* further argues that ordinary people become capable of extraordinary violence not due to inherent pathology, but rather because of systemic forces, social pressures, and ideological justifications. This reinforces the idea that psychological mechanisms must be analyzed within their social and historical context.

Situational Enablers (Cohen & Felson)

Routine Activity Theory (Cohen & Felson, 1979) provides a criminological lens for understanding how sexual violence during the Partition was facilitated by the breakdown of societal norms and law enforcement structures. According to this theory, violence becomes more likely when three elements converge: a motivated offender, a suitable target, and the absence of a capable guardian. The collapse of British colonial authority, the disintegration of police and military oversight, and the mass displacement of people created a vacuum in which sexual violence could be committed with impunity.

This framework is particularly valuable in understanding why sexual violence escalated so dramatically during the Partition. The sudden collapse of colonial law enforcement meant that perpetrators faced few immediate consequences. The hurried and chaotic exit of British forces created a power vacuum, especially in rural and border regions where local police either disbanded or stood by passively as violence unfolded. The lawlessness bred by this institutional void made sexual violence not just possible but frequent and expected. As Menon and Bhasin argue, even the post-Partition state struggled to address these crimes, often prioritizing diplomatic recovery over justice for victims (Menon & Bhasin, 1998).

Displacement also contributed significantly to the opportunity structure. Refugee convoys, trains, and camps became prime targets for sexual violence due to their vulnerability. Women were separated from their families or forced to flee under duress and were frequently abducted or assaulted along the way. The dehumanizing conditions of transit—marked by exhaustion, lack of shelter, and overcrowding—stripped away protective barriers and placed women directly in harm's way. Testimonies collected by the 1947 Partition Archive recount numerous instances where women were pulled from trains or refugee lines and attacked with little intervention.

In addition, the ideological framing of the Partition as a moment of existential crisis created the perception that acts of extreme violence were not only permissible but necessary. In such a climate, perpetrators believed they were acting in defense of their faith, family, or homeland. The absence of legal deterrents combined with the presence of ideological justifications created a potent recipe for impunity. As James Waller notes, situational pressures can transform the ordinary into the extraordinary, especially when societal norms are disrupted and violence becomes an expected form of communal expression (Waller, 2002).

Government documents from India, such as *The Abducted Persons (Recovery and Restoration) Act of 1949*, show that thousands of abductions occurred during and after the Partition, many of which involved forced conversions and marriages. These were not random acts but occurred in a context where violence was normalized, law was absent, and perpetrators faced little or no accountability.

Gendered Violence in Ethnic Conflicts (Sharlach, Das)

Although this study does not center on a gender analysis-based method, it draws from Lisa Sharlach's *Rape as Genocide (2000)* and Veena Das's *Life and Words (2007)* to contextualize sexual violence as a tool of ethnic domination and revenge. Sharlach's work on the Rwandan and Bosnian genocides argues that rape is not simply a byproduct of war but a strategy for terrorizing communities and asserting dominance. Similarly, Das demonstrates how acts of violence become embedded in everyday life and memory, reshaping individual and collective identities.

What distinguishes the Partition from other instances of wartime sexual violence is the scale and social complicity with which these acts were committed. Drawing from Sharlach's analysis, sexual violence in Rwanda and Bosnia during their genocides was often explicitly organized and encouraged by state or paramilitary forces. In the Partition, however, while not state-directed, the violence was socially sanctioned within communities. The use of sexual violence as a symbolic assertion of dominance was normalized through everyday discourse and reinforced by a lack of accountability. Veena Das emphasizes in her ethnographic work that violence becomes part of everyday life not just through repetition, but through the social narratives that make it intelligible (Das, 2007). During the Partition, stories of revenge and honor circulated widely, framing the sexual violation of the other as just and necessary.

The symbolic nature of these violations extended beyond the individual victim. Women were often abducted and forced into marriages or conversions to demonstrate the erasure of an entire community's cultural identity. These acts, though deeply personal, were treated as public and communal victories or defeats. Das's notion that violence lives on in the silences and broken narratives of survivors is particularly applicable here—many women were never able to return or reintegrate into their communities, having been marked as dishonored or defiled by that very community. This reflects the long-term psychological and societal damage that sexual violence inflicts, both on individuals and collective memory.

While this study intentionally avoids framing the Partition's sexual violence solely through a gendered lens, it acknowledges that the gendered dimension cannot be entirely separated from ethnic conflict, especially given the gendered nature of this violence. The gendered lens is instrumental to Partition-related violence and will be explored in-depth in future studies. Women's bodies were sites on which ethnic boundaries were drawn and contested. Sharlach's argument that rape functions as an act of symbolic erasure in ethnic conflict is essential to understanding the stakes of these crimes during the Partition. The goal was not merely to violate, but to unmake identity—to transform the victim into something unrecognizable to their original community.

The Partition's sexual violence mirrors these patterns. Women and children were abducted, raped, and forcibly converted to erase the presence of the "enemy" and symbolically desecrate the community. Political and religious leaders used rhetoric that made these acts appear acceptable—or even heroic.

Synthesis: Interlocking Mechanisms of Violence

This synthesis affirms that the convergence of cognitive, emotional, and social factors produced an environment in which violence could be justified, performed, and even celebrated. Each theoretical lens highlights one component of this transformation, but their combined effect lies in how they function dynamically. For example, moral disengagement allowed perpetrators to construct a mental and emotional distance from their actions, but this distancing was often enhanced by the dehumanization processes operating simultaneously in the cultural and political discourse. Group conformity added yet another layer, validating those rationalizations through communal reinforcement.

In the Partition context, perpetrators did not act in psychological vacuums—they were embedded in networks of peers, leaders, rumors, and grievances. Rumors of sexual atrocities committed by the "other side" often served as emotional triggers, fueling cycles of retaliatory violence. The spread of these narratives through community elders, religious leaders, and local newspapers meant that perpetrators felt not only morally justified but morally compelled to act. These local ideologies and circulating stories amplified existing psychological mechanisms, showing how emotion, cognition, and structure aligned to erode moral barriers to violence.

Furthermore, the convergence of opportunity and ideology was a key accelerant in the translation of justification into action. The lack of legal enforcement and oversight created what Cohen and Felson call a "criminogenic environment," in which even individuals with weak ideological commitments could be swept into patterns of sexual violence (Cohen & Felson, 1979). These patterns were made all the more likely by the symbolic weight assigned to women's bodies as bearers of communal honor, transforming violence against individuals into attacks on identity and group cohesion.

What emerges from the discussion above is a multifaceted explanation of sexual violence that challenges both singular causality and narrow disciplinary lenses. Each of the theoretical frameworks explored—moral disengagement, dehumanization, group conformity, situational enablers, and symbolic violence in ethnic conflict—sheds light on a specific aspect of the conditions that enabled mass sexual violence during the Partition. However, these mechanisms did not operate in isolation. Instead, they interacted in mutually reinforcing ways that transformed moral transgression into social expectation.

For instance, dehumanization was not only a psychological precondition for violence, but also reinforced the diffusion of responsibility in group settings. When victims were stripped of their personhood, they were no longer seen as individuals but as representatives of an enemy group. This abstraction made it easier for perpetrators to commit acts of sexual violence without guilt, especially in the presence of peer pressure. Similarly, moral justification operated at the level of individual cognition and was reinforced through communal narratives, rumors, and media rhetoric, enabling violence to appear socially sanctioned and even valorized.

The convergence of opportunity theory and psychological theory is particularly powerful in the Partition context. The collapse of British authority, combined with mass refugee flows and a lack of legal deterrents, created the ideal conditions for ordinary individuals to commit extraordinary crimes. These crimes were often preceded by ideological framing and moral disengagement, and facilitated through group dynamics and situational anonymity. The frameworks explored in this chapter therefore provide a conceptual toolkit for analyzing perpetrator behavior that is historically grounded and translatable across different regions.

Looking Forward: Regional Application of the Framework

Each regional context offers unique social, political, and historical conditions that shaped how psychological mechanisms manifested in acts of violence. For instance, in Punjab, the intensity and scale of communal clashes were magnified by the sheer speed of population transfer and the collapse of local governance, creating a volatile setting for mob-led sexual violence. Bengal, by contrast, experienced more localized and urban-based violence, where political propaganda and pre-existing communal fissures fueled moral disengagement in different ways. In Sindh and Kashmir, the legacy of princely state governance, tribal loyalties, and uneven administrative control shaped how group conformity and situational enablers contributed to sexual aggression.

Analyzing these regional variations allows for a nuanced understanding of how broader psychological frameworks must be adapted to local conditions. While the theoretical lens remains consistent, its specific application requires attention to context-specific variables—such as the presence of state actors, regional media discourses, and communal histories—when examining the dynamics of conflict. This comparative approach does not suggest equivalency in the experience or scale of violence, but rather emphasizes the adaptability and recurrence of these psychological mechanisms in diverse communal environments.

Furthermore, a regional analysis enhances the study's contribution to the field of comparative genocide and mass violence studies by underscoring the importance of micro-histories. These localized stories resist monolithic narratives and instead illuminate how mass violence is experienced, interpreted, and remembered differently depending on one's social and geographic position. Through this approach, the study not only explains how psychological theories operate on a structural level but also attends to the lived realities and testimonies that bring these theories into sharp and often painful focus.

Chapter 2 will apply this integrated theoretical framework to a set of regional case studies. By analyzing how moral disengagement and situational enablers functioned across different areas—Punjab, Bengal, Sindh, and Kashmir—this study will demonstrate that these psychological processes were not unique to one context but were replicated across a range of communal settings. The goal is not only to understand *how* violence occurred but *why* ordinary individuals believed it was justifiable and necessary.

The regional case studies will also allow for a deeper engagement with survivor testimonies, government documents, and media sources, showing how violence was contextualized differently depending on local dynamics but often followed strikingly similar psychological patterns. In doing so, the study seeks to contribute not only to the historiography of the Partition, but also to broader theories of mass violence, ethnic conflict, and perpetrator psychology.

CHAPTER 2

HISTORICAL CONTEXT – SEXUAL VIOLENCE IN THE PARTITION ACROSS REGIONS

Building on the conceptual foundation established in Chapter 1, this chapter examines how the psychological mechanisms of moral disengagement, dehumanization, and group conformity manifested through specific regional experiences of Partition violence. The central argument is that while the conditions of the Partition varied across geographies, the processes through which sexual violence was enabled and justified followed consistent psychological trajectories. Regional diversity did not prevent the recurrence of patterns; rather, it revealed how local conditions influenced the expression of the same underlying cognitive and social dynamics.

In addressing each region, this chapter analyzes how perpetrators framed their actions through local rhetoric, communal memory, and cultural scripts of honor and revenge. It also considers how the breakdown of legal and administrative institutions influenced group behavior, fostering impunity and heightening emotional triggers. While the forms of violence—rape, abduction, forced conversion—remained largely consistent, the language, justifications, and social reinforcement that enabled them differed across Punjab, Bengal, Sindh, and Kashmir. By tracing these differences and similarities, this chapter aims to demonstrate the broad applicability of the psychological framework developed earlier while also attending to the historical specificity of each locale.

This chapter examines the regional diversity of sexual violence during the 1947 Partition of India by analyzing four major zones of conflict: Punjab, Bengal, Sindh, and Kashmir. The goal is to apply the theoretical frameworks established in Chapter 1—particularly moral disengagement, dehumanization, and situational enablers—within historically grounded regional case studies. Each case highlights how different communal dynamics, demographic patterns, political leadership, and media discourse shaped the forms and frequency of sexual violence. While these regions experienced varying scales and intensities of violence, the psychological and structural mechanisms that enabled it were strikingly consistent.

Punjab

The Epicenter of Partition Violence

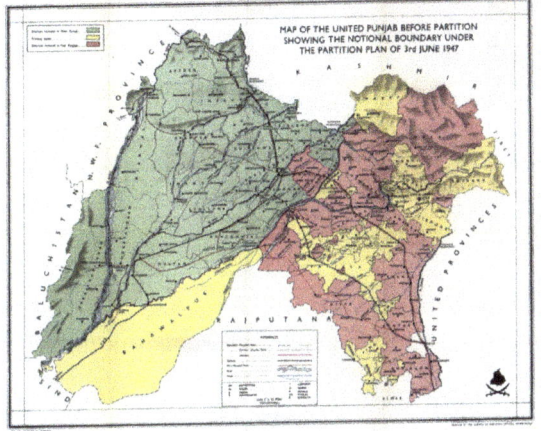

United Punjab before Partition, showing notional boundary under the Partition Plan, 3 June 1947. Reprinted *From Survey of Pakistan Offices, Rawalpindi, 1947.* Public domain.

One additional factor that distinguished Punjab's violence was the mobilization of religious imagery to justify and sanctify sexual violence. Religious leaders and local influencers often invoked narratives of holy war, suggesting that defending the faith required the domination and humiliation of enemy women. As Das points out, "violence during Partition was often couched in the language of purification and moral duty, not mere vengeance" (Das, 2007, p. 62). This religious framing provided an additional layer of moral disengagement, allowing perpetrators to interpret their actions as spiritually endorsed rather than ethically problematic.

The physical geography of Punjab—marked by vast open fields, mobile refugee convoys, and rural isolation—also played a crucial role. These landscapes provided ideal situational enablers by creating liminal zones beyond the reach of fragmented state authority. The rural expanses between towns became theaters of unregulated violence, where women were particularly vulnerable (Khan, 2007, p. 144). The very nature of the refugee movement, fragmented and exposed, amplified the opportunities for communal violence and sexual domination.

Furthermore, it is critical to examine how symbolic acts of violence in Punjab were designed to reverberate across community memory. Acts such as forcing survivors to carry religious flags of the opposing community or branding them with religious symbols served not just to humiliate the individual but to broadcast a warning to an entire community. This strategy mirrors Smith's argument that violence against the dehumanized is intended as a message to the living as much as a punishment for the victim (Smith, 2011, p. 126). Such acts ensured that the violence would endure as psychological terror within both the victim's and the survivor's collective consciousness.

Another critical factor in Punjab was the normalization of mob justice. In many refugee convoys and border towns, local leaders and influential figures either condoned or encouraged collective retribution. Group moral disengagement is sustained when leaders mobilize selective moral justifications (Bandura, 1999, p. 207). The repeated invocation of group loyalty, honor, and historical grievance fostered an environment where sexual violence could be reframed as a public service to one's community. The moral burden was not individually carried; it was collectivized and thus psychologically diluted among perpetrators.

The trauma experienced by survivors in Punjab also carried distinct intergenerational consequences. Testimonies collected decades later reveal that women who were abducted, raped, or forcibly converted often faced permanent exile from their families and communities. This pattern highlights how the initial act of violence was compounded by prolonged societal rejection—a form of secondary victimization that reinforced communal moral disengagement. Violence extends beyond the event itself into the social reconstitution of identity and exclusion (Das, 2007, p. 85).

Moreover, the spectacle of violence became a tool for communal signaling. Public rapes and abductions served as warnings to rival communities, asserting both physical dominance and psychological superiority. Survivors report being paraded through towns or forcibly displayed at border posts, transforming acts of sexual violence into communal rituals of terror. This public nature of violence amplified its psychological impact, ensuring that fear, humiliation, and subjugation were individual experiences and collective traumas etched into community memory.

Understanding the psychological and situational elements specific to Punjab requires attention to the region's rapid political unraveling. As Talbot and Singh explain, the sudden shift from British colonial governance to the sovereign administrations of India and Pakistan occurred without adequate planning or enforcement capacity, particularly along the newly drawn borders (Talbot & Singh, 2009, p. 66). Administrative breakdown created a context in which violence was not just allowed but, in many cases, expected. The abrupt transformation of previously interdependent communities into adversaries left little time for reconciliation or trust-building.

The mass migration itself played a central role in enabling the psychological mechanisms outlined in Chapter 1. The forced movement of millions resulted in the creation of liminal, lawless spaces—train stations, refugee camps, open roads—where norms could be suspended. Cohen and Felson's Routine Activity Theory becomes highly relevant in this context. The sudden exposure of vulnerable populations, combined with the absence of capable guardians, made conditions ideal for perpetrators to act with impunity. Women and children in flight were particularly vulnerable, not just physically but symbolically, as targets of communal retribution.

Additionally, emotional catalysts such as grief, humiliation, and vengeance were omnipresent in Punjab. Testimonies from survivors and witnesses, collected by the 1947 Partition Archive, frequently mention that men justified their participation in acts of sexual violence as direct responses to what they heard had been done to "their women." This cycle of retributive violence was not only allowed by community leaders but often incited by them, creating an emotional and social environment in which violence felt righteous rather than reprehensible. In this context, Bandura's theory of moral justification intersects directly with Waller's observation that people often commit violence not because of hatred but because of perceived moral obligation (Waller, 2007, p. 89).

No region experienced the upheaval of the Partition as intensely as Punjab. The Radcliffe Line split the province down the middle, resulting in one of the largest and most chaotic migrations in human history. More than 15 million people were displaced, and an estimated one million were killed. As Yasmin Khan notes in *The Great Partition (2007)*, "Punjab was where the Partition became a cataclysm rather than a bureaucratic act" (Khan, 2007, p. 135).

Sexual violence in Punjab was systematic and often executed with symbolic intention. Women were abducted from refugee caravans and trains, raped in public, and in many cases, forced to convert and marry across religious lines. Menon and Bhasin's *Borders & Boundaries (1998)* present harrowing testimonies from abducted women in Punjab, including one survivor who recalled, "They said they would take me as a prize for their village because I was the daughter of a prominent Hindu" (Menon & Bhasin, 1998, p. 103). The symbolic targeting of women from elite or respected families reflects the role of sexual violence as an act of communal domination, not merely individual impulse.

From a psychological standpoint, moral disengagement in Punjab was reinforced by deeply entrenched communal ideologies. Rape and abduction were often framed as acts of justice or reciprocity. Khan recounts that many perpetrators viewed their actions as necessary for avenging women on "their side" who had suffered similar fates (Khan, 2007, p. 141). This circular logic of communal honor allowed perpetrators to morally justify their actions and emotionally detach from the human suffering they caused.

The collapse of law enforcement and administrative authority in Punjab created ideal conditions for situational enablers to flourish. The British exit left a power vacuum, and both nascent Indian and Pakistani forces were unable—or unwilling—to control the mobs. This environment of impunity allowed sexual violence to be carried out with little fear of consequence. Government records from *The Abducted Persons (Recovery and Restoration) Act, 1949* reveal that thousands of women were still missing years after the Partition, many never recovered due to resistance from their captors or their own communities (GOI, 1949).

Fractured Identities | 111

Bengal

Urban Centers and the Role of Political Rhetoric

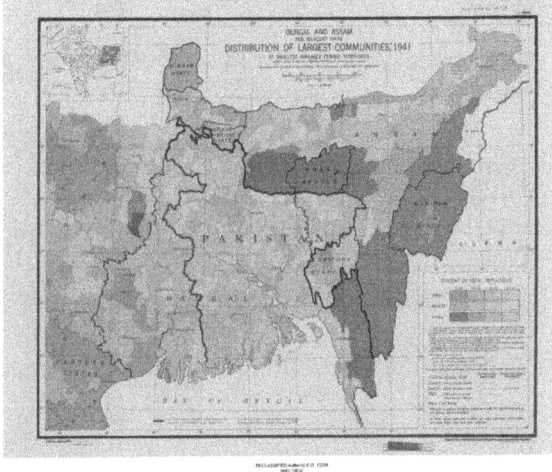

Bengal and Assam, distribution of largest communities, 1941. Based on the 1941 Census of India. Published by the Survey of India, 1944. Public domain.

Political pamphlets and speeches during the Partition in Bengal often invoked past grievances to fuel cycles of revenge. Menon and Bhasin note that "urban centers became saturated with stories of victimization, creating a moral landscape where retaliation was framed as communal obligation" (Menon & Bhasin, 1998, p. 104). Such narrative inflation heightened group identities while suppressing empathy for the 'other,' a classic facilitator of dehumanization.

Urban anonymity in Bengal also produced a distinct kind of impunity. Unlike the close-knit rural communities where perpetrators risked social censure, cities allowed attackers to operate without fear of recognition. As Browning notes, "Anonymity within large populations weakens individual moral agency and strengthens situational conformity" (Browning, 1992, p. 78). In Kolkata and Dhaka, mobs could form, commit atrocities, and disperse without accountability, making the psychological barriers to violence even lower.

Moreover, local media in Bengal played a decisive role in framing sexual violence as part of a broader struggle for political autonomy. Newspapers sensationalized communal violence, framing women's bodies as territories to be captured, violated, or redeemed. According to Das, "language acts as both a medium of violence and a repository of its normalization" (Das, 2007, p. 59). In this way, euphemistic labeling and emotional triggers were socially tolerated and actively cultivated.

Bengal's dense urban centers created different conditions for violence, where rumors and propaganda could spread rapidly through newspapers, street sermons, and public rallies. Urban anonymity allowed perpetrators to operate without the inhibiting gaze of a familiar village community, leading to an escalation in brutal and performative violence. The emotional proximity to political movements, often manipulated by opportunistic leaders, created an atmosphere where violence was imbued with ideological legitimacy. As Khan argues, "Partition violence in Bengal became a performance of competing nationalisms" (Khan, 2007, p. 155).

In contrast to the village-based violence of Punjab, Bengal's sexual assaults were often intertwined with lootings, property seizures, and arson—acts that collectively signaled territorial reassertion. These accompanying acts reinforced the idea that violence against women was part of a broader strategy to erase the enemy's presence and claim symbolic victory. Religious processions, market gatherings, and even household spaces were transformed into sites of gendered brutality, showcasing how urban structures were repurposed for communal dominance.

Additionally, the reaction of the police and judiciary in Bengal further entrenched patterns of impunity. Testimonies reveal that victims who approached police stations were often dismissed or threatened into silence. The legal system's failure to prosecute perpetrators served as a tacit endorsement of moral disengagement, signaling to communities that sexual violence was an acceptable extension of political conflict. This institutional abdication mirrored Bandura's insight that "official sanctioning or tacit consent from authorities weakens internal moral restraints against violent conduct" (Bandura, 1999, p. 211).

Unlike Punjab, Bengal's Partition was marked less by mass migration and more by administrative confusion, leading to a different but equally insidious pattern of sexual violence. Bengal's communal tensions were inflamed in urban centers like Calcutta and Dhaka, where political and media discourse helped justify and spread fear. As Ayesha Jalal observes, "In Bengal, the everyday became a battleground for ideological contest, where even the most mundane interactions could erupt into political violence" (Jalal, 2013, p. 119).

In Bengal, sexual violence took the form of targeted assaults and communal riots. Religious rhetoric and political manipulation were instrumental in fostering moral disengagement. Das's *Life and Words (2007)* emphasizes how rumors of rape and abduction were used as psychological tools to incite collective fear and justification for revenge attacks: "The story of a girl raped became the story of a community dishonored, legitimizing acts of equal or greater brutality" (Das, 2007, p. 53). This weaponization of emotion enabled ordinary individuals to engage in horrific acts, believing them to be morally and communally sanctioned.

Theoretical mechanisms like euphemistic labeling and dehumanization were visible in Bengal through newspaper headlines and public discourse. *The Statesman*, one of the most widely circulated English-language newspapers, often employed language that framed victims as casualties of necessary retaliation. These rhetorical patterns sanitized the violence and contributed to a communal moral code that normalized sexual assault.

As in Punjab, the disintegration of state authority played a key role in enabling sexual violence. The Partition in Bengal was slower and bureaucratically entangled, creating pockets of insecurity in which mobs acted with a sense of entitlement. The lack of legal accountability, combined with media-fueled emotional triggers, allowed violence to become both performative and pervasive.

The urban nature of violence in Bengal also meant that incidents of sexual assault were often carried out in highly visible, public settings—frequently in marketplaces, streets, or near places of worship. This performativity was not incidental; it served to humiliate communities and send clear messages of power, dominance, and communal revenge. As Menon and Bhasin document, "The visibility of sexual violence was meant to signal the destruction of the other's honor, not just the defilement of the body" (Menon & Bhasin, 1998, p. 111). This aligns with Smith's framework of dehumanization, as violence became a performative ritual to erase human identity and replace it with symbolic meaning.

Bengal's political leadership also played a role in either enabling or failing to prevent sexual violence. According to Jalal, there was a notable hesitation among elites to publicly acknowledge the severity of sexual violence, partly due to fears of further inflaming communal tensions (Jalal,

2013, p. 122). This institutional silence functioned as a form of passive endorsement, creating what Waller describes as an "ambient permission" in which perpetrators felt no social or legal pressure to restrain themselves (Waller, 2007, p. 96). The state's failure to intervene effectively allowed psychological mechanisms like moral justification and displacement of responsibility to operate unchallenged.

Furthermore, Bengal's complex religious demography—comprising Hindus, Muslims, and other minority groups—meant that sexual violence often carried intersecting motives. While communal identity remained a primary vector of violence, caste and class divisions also influenced who was targeted. Das notes, "The violence was filtered through local systems of power, and sexual assault became a way to assert not just religious dominance, but also gender and class hierarchies" (Das, 2007, p. 57). These intersecting layers of identity added further psychological rationalization, deepening the moral disengagement of perpetrators who saw their victims not just as members of an enemy religion but as socially inferior or expendable.

Sindh

Forced Conversions and Political Opportunism

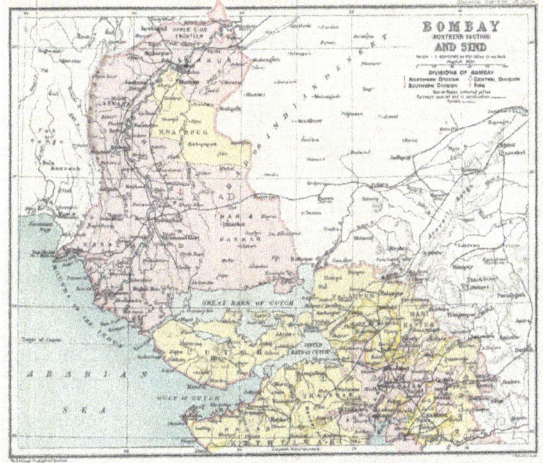

Bombay (Northern Section and Sind), 1909. Reprinted from *Imperial Gazetteer of India: Atlas.* Oxford Clarendon Press. Public domain.

A major difference in Sindh's pattern of violence was the way political opportunism merged with religious zeal. As Talbot and Singh note, "local elites often manipulated communal tensions to consolidate land and economic power, disguising their opportunism under the rhetoric of religious duty" (Talbot & Singh, 2009, p. 93). This convergence created an environment where abductions and conversions were framed not only as pious acts but also as necessary components of socio-economic reordering.

The manipulation of religious rituals to normalize sexual violence in Sindh was further bolstered by peer pressure within tribal communities. Browning's study suggests that "perpetrators in close-knit units often felt compelled to conform to group behaviors to avoid social ostracism" (Browning, 1992, p. 81). In Sindh's tribal networks, the expectation to participate in forced conversions and marriages became a critical mechanism of moral disengagement.

Additionally, the involvement of religious courts in legitimizing these acts blurred the boundary between communal justice and sexual exploitation. When harmful acts are given institutional blessing, individuals find it easier to disengage morally from their behavior (Bandura, 1999, p. 210). The legal apparatus in Sindh, complicit or silent, allowed perpetrators to see their actions as socially sanctioned rather than criminal.

The cultural fabric of Sindh, with its complex layering of tribal customs and Islamic revivalist movements, created an environment where religious identity became a primary lens for both communal belonging and exclusion. During the Partition, this focus was weaponized through the ritualization of forced conversions and marriages, transforming deeply personal traumas into public affirmations of communal dominance. Survivors' testimonies reveal that many women were renamed, forcibly re-clothed in religious symbols, and presented in public ceremonies to mark their 'purification.' This symbolic erasure of identity echoes Sharlach's argument that "ethnic and gendered violence seeks not only to destroy individuals but to rewrite communal narratives" (Sharlach, 2000, p. 85).

The role of local clerics and community elders in legitimizing forced conversions in Sindh further highlights the interplay between religious authority and moral disengagement. In many cases, clerics were called upon to officiate sham marriages, providing a thin veneer of religious sanctity to what were fundamentally acts of abduction and coercion. As Bandura explains, "legitimizing harmful conduct under the guise of religious or moral righteousness enables perpetrators to absolve themselves from personal accountability" (Bandura, 1999, p. 212). The collaboration of religious leaders thus entrenched moral disengagement not merely at the individual level but across entire communal institutions.

Moreover, Sindh's relatively slower, more organized exodus allowed for the strategic targeting of Hindu women rather than the chaotic, opportunistic violence seen elsewhere. Testimonies from survivors suggest that many abductions were premeditated, with lists drawn up of desirable victims based on wealth, caste, or perceived communal status. This systemic aspect of violence in Sindh reveals that sexual aggression was reactive and a planned dimension of social reordering, crafted to eliminate minority influence and bolster emergent national identities.

Tribal politics, delayed migration, and the consolidation of Pakistani identity shaped the experience of the Partition in Sindh. Unlike Punjab or Bengal, where violence occurred at the point of exodus, in Sindh, it was often delayed, erupting as Hindu communities began to evacuate in the months following independence. Ian Talbot and Gurharpal Singh note, "The exodus of Hindus from Sindh was not caused solely by violence but by the slow suffocation of civic life through harassment and intimidation" (Talbot & Singh, 2009, p. 89).

In Sindh, sexual violence was deeply entwined with the project of forced religious conversion. Hindu women were often abducted, converted to Islam, and forcibly married. These actions were framed as acts of religious salvation or patriotic duty. The psychological mechanism of moral justification is crucial here. As one captured woman reported in a government recovery file, "They said they were saving me from the shame of being a kafir" (GOI, 1949). This language reflects both moral disengagement and dehumanization—where violence was reframed as a benevolent act.

The tribal and feudal structures of Sindh also reinforced situational enablers. Many perpetrators acted with the knowledge that local leaders or influential landowners protected them.

This dynamic aligns with Browning and Waller's assertions that peer and authority structures not only condone but promote violence through group norms and expectations. Because the perpetrators in Sindh often had economic or political ties to regional elites, impunity became a structural rather than circumstantial phenomenon.

Religious framing in Sindh was uniquely potent, as conversion was not merely enforced but publicly celebrated as part of the nation-building process. Public ceremonies often marked these conversions, reinforcing communal narratives that framed such acts as patriotic rather than violent. This public endorsement contributed to euphemistic labeling, a key component of moral disengagement, by framing coerced sexual relationships as moral or redemptive. As Bandura notes, such language reshapes the moral evaluation of acts, making it easier for perpetrators to justify their behavior (Bandura, 1999, p. 75).

The slow exodus of Hindu families also meant that violence often occurred in more intimate, personal settings rather than chaotic public spaces. Unlike the mass attacks seen on refugee trains in Punjab, abductions in Sindh often occurred within villages or neighborhoods, blurring the line between private and public spheres. This created a different form of psychological insulation for perpetrators—actions took on the character of localized enforcement rather than opportunistic violence. The familiarity between victim and perpetrator in many of these cases added another layer of moral disengagement through the personalization of ideology.

Additionally, the political leadership in Sindh failed to condemn or curb these abuses, often downplaying them as isolated incidents or dismissing them as byproducts of transition. This state silence not only fostered impunity but further reinforced the notion that these acts were in alignment with the national interest. As Talbot and Singh argue, "The Pakistani state's ambiguous stance toward violence in Sindh allowed religious and ethnic motives to be exercised freely in the name of security and reform" (Talbot & Singh, 2009, p. 91). It created a feedback loop where inaction was interpreted as approval, deepening the cycle of justification and abuse.

Kashmir

Territorial Conflict and the Gendered Battlefield

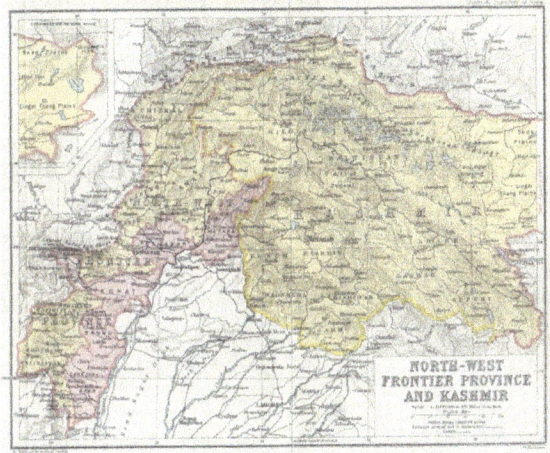

North-West Frontier Province and Kashmir, 1909. Reprinted from *Imperial Gazetteer of India: Atlas.* Oxford: Clarendon Press. Public domain.

Psychological terror in Kashmir was reinforced through strategies of symbolic erasure. Women were not only abducted but often forcibly renamed, converted, and re-ritualized into the identity of the dominant group. This echoes Smith's assertion that "dehumanization involves not just physical harm but the obliteration of a victim's social identity" (Smith, 2011, p. 143). The erasure of original identities in Kashmir was thus both a personal and communal conquest.

The strategic use of sexual violence to facilitate demographic change in Kashmir mirrored broader patterns of ethnic cleansing seen elsewhere. Sharlach notes, "sexual violence is employed systematically to make a community's continued presence in a contested area psychologically unbearable" (Sharlach, 2000, p. 88). In Kashmir, this tactic not only displaced populations but left lasting scars on the cultural memory of those regions.

Lastly, the silence from emerging state authorities in Kashmir reinforced the normalization of sexual violence. Talbot and Singh argue that "both the Indian and Pakistani authorities had vested interests in minimizing reports of atrocities to maintain political legitimacy" (Talbot & Singh, 2009, p. 165). This suppression of acknowledgment allowed perpetrators to feel shielded by nationalist goals, further embedding moral disengagement within the evolving nation-building projects on both sides.

One distinctive feature of sexual violence in Kashmir was the strategic use of rape to facilitate demographic engineering. Reports indicate that certain tribal militias targeted specific villages for mass rape and abduction to encourage Hindu and Sikh populations to flee, effectively altering the religious composition of contested territories.

This strategy reflects Sharlach's assertion that sexual violence can serve as a tactic of forced displacement, aimed at achieving both psychological and territorial conquest (Sharlach, 2000, p. 87).

In Kashmir, the spatial isolation of many communities amplified the psychological terror inflicted by sexual violence. Villages surrounded by forests, mountains, and rivers found themselves cut off from external support or intervention, exacerbating feelings of abandonment and hopelessness among victims. The remoteness made it difficult for survivors to seek help or justice, ensuring that the violence remained hidden and unpunished. This dynamic highlights how geography can serve as a situational enabler, a factor often overlooked in more urban-centric analyses of Partition violence.

The symbolic dimension of Kashmir's gendered violence reverberated through nationalist discourses on both sides of the border. Women's bodies became metaphors for the territory itself—violated, contested, and symbolically reclaimed. The abduction or rescue of women was often portrayed in public narratives as equivalent to the loss or preservation of Kashmir itself. This symbolic coding of gendered violence reinforced communal grievances and perpetuated cycles of moral disengagement, embedding the logic of Partition violence into the nationalist imaginations of both India and Pakistan for decades to come.

The violence in Kashmir occurred against the backdrop of unresolved territorial disputes and cross-border military incursions. The tribal invasion of Kashmir in late 1947 led to a series of atrocities, including mass rapes and abductions of women. According to Khan, "The assault on Kashmir was seen not just as a military conquest but a reclamation of space and identity—women's bodies were conscripted into this project" (Khan, 2007, p. 174).

Unlike the communal riots in Punjab and Bengal, sexual violence in Kashmir was carried out in the context of paramilitary offensives. These structured military incursions borrowed heavily from the psychological frameworks discussed in Chapter 1. Milgram and Waller's work on obedience and authority is particularly relevant here: perpetrators acted under the command of tribal leaders or military figures, allowing them to diffuse responsibility and suppress guilt.

Kashmir's remote geography and militarized environment created ideal conditions for moral disengagement. Victims were often portrayed in propaganda as traitors, collaborators, or symbols of enemy rule. This process of symbolic dehumanization rendered sexual violence as a means of punishing not just individuals but entire populations. As Sharlach argues in *Rape as Genocide (2000)*, "Rape becomes genocidal when it aims not merely to harm but to permanently alter the cultural fabric of a group" (Sharlach, 2000, p. 81). In Kashmir, this was evident in the targeting of minority women in villages known for their political or religious affiliations.

This targeting was not merely tactical but deeply ideological. Sexual violence became a method of rewriting communal boundaries, as the abduction and forced assimilation of women were used to assert dominance over contested populations. This form of identity erasure echoes David Livingstone Smith's theory that dehumanization allows perpetrators to perceive their victims as "less than human," and therefore outside the moral order (Smith, 2011, p. 158). In Kashmir, the erasure of women's identities—through forced conversions, name changes, and assimilation into tribal communities—was framed as both religious purification and political conquest.

These acts of sexual violence were also facilitated by an absence of state oversight, much like in Punjab and Sindh. However, in Kashmir, the absence was more profound due to its remote geography and the contested nature of its sovereignty. The chaos surrounding the princely state's accession to India left entire regions ungoverned and exposed to militarized violence (Talbot & Singh, 2009, p. 163). This allowed tribal militias and other non-state actors to operate with impunity, further enabling the psychological mechanisms of moral disengagement, euphemistic labeling, and dehumanization.

Furthermore, Kashmir exemplifies how territorial conflicts create conditions for sexual violence that are both immediate and systemic. While individuals committed acts of rape and abduction, they were embedded within a broader strategic vision. This aligns with Lisa Sharlach's contention that rape in the context of ethnic conflict is often used to achieve military objectives through psychological and demographic destabilization (Sharlach, 2000, p. 83). In Kashmir, the use of sexual violence served not just to inflict trauma but to permanently alter the demographic and cultural makeup of targeted regions.

Case Study Synthesis

Despite the geographic, cultural, and demographic differences among Punjab, Bengal, Sindh, and Kashmir, the psychological mechanisms underpinning the Partition's sexual violence—moral disengagement, dehumanization, group conformity, and situational enablers—remained disturbingly consistent. Across diverse settings, perpetrators found ways to frame violence as duty, honor, or religious salvation, revealing a grim universality in the cognitive processes that underwrite mass atrocity. These regional case studies collectively demonstrate that the Partition's violence was not random chaos but a structured phenomenon shaped by recognizable psychological and social forces. As the next chapter will explore, understanding how perpetrators justified their actions—through language, ritual, and silence—is critical to comprehending how mass sexual violence was sustained, normalized, and embedded into communal memory.

CHAPTER 3

PERPETRATOR JUSTIFICATIONS AND MORAL DISENGAGEMENT

Chapter 3 investigates how perpetrators of sexual violence during the 1947 Partition of India rationalized and justified their actions, thereby engaging in the process of moral disengagement. While the previous chapters established the theoretical basis and regional application of these mechanisms, this chapter examines the ways in which such cognitive processes were verbalized, disseminated, and reinforced socially. Through survivor testimonies, newspaper discourse, religious rhetoric, and state silence, perpetrators developed psychological buffers that enabled them to participate in or condone violence without experiencing guilt. This process was not spontaneous; rather, it was cultivated over time through narratives of victimhood, honor, and historical grievance. Perpetrators did not act in isolation—they were influenced by peers, religious leaders, and political rhetoric that collectively redefined violence as a communal duty. These justifications were reinforced by widespread silence or implicit approval, contributing to the normalization of sexual violence during the Partition. Understanding how individuals made sense of their actions allows us to uncover the cultural and psychological scaffolding that made mass atrocities possible and how perpetrators of sexual violence during the 1947 Partition of India rationalized and justified their actions, thereby engaging in the process of moral disengagement.

Moreover, this chapter examines how such rationalizations were not fleeting moments of convenience, but rather enduring belief systems deeply embedded in personal memory and collective storytelling. The chapter also interrogates how violence was not only permitted by these frameworks but ritualized—ritualized in the performance of group conformity, in the cadence of revenge narratives, and in the silence of institutions meant to administer justice. The cumulative effect of these factors constructed a moral landscape where perpetrators not only distanced themselves from wrongdoing but also reimagined themselves as moral agents of their community's defense. In this context, moral disengagement becomes not simply a psychological process, but a social project—one that relies on repetition, silence, and communal complicity. By tracing the deployment of these justifications across multiple sources, this chapter aims to reconstruct the mental universe of perpetrators. Only by understanding these mental landscapes can scholars begin to explain how ordinary people come to commit acts of extraordinary violence. These insights also inform broader conversations about memory, accountability, and the psychological legacies of mass violence that continue long after the physical violence has ceased.

Albert Bandura's theory of moral disengagement explains that people morally disengage from harmful acts through various cognitive mechanisms such as moral justification, euphemistic labeling, dehumanization, and diffusion of responsibility. People do not ordinarily engage in harmful conduct until they have justified to themselves the morality of their actions (Bandura, 1999, p. 193). In the context of the Partition, moral disengagement was often articulated through narratives of communal revenge, religious duty, and the restoration of honor. These justifications not only facilitated individual participation in sexual violence but also created collective environments in which such acts were socially sanctioned. These mechanisms are particularly relevant in the context of the Partition, where traditional moral systems collapsed amidst extreme political upheaval. Violence against women, especially, was not just tolerated but encouraged as a means of asserting communal superiority. Bandura's insights contextualize how perpetrators could maintain a sense of moral integrity even while committing acts of extraordinary cruelty. The theory further explains how moral disengagement functions not only at the individual level but also collectively, through cultural norms and shared beliefs.

Survivor testimonies are perhaps the most poignant evidence of how perpetrators rationalized their actions. In *Borders & Boundaries (1998)*, Menon and Bhasin document the words of a survivor whose captor declared, "What we do is not wrong. Your men did this to our women. This is God's justice" (Menon & Bhasin, 1998, p. 114). This invocation of divine retribution transforms a brutal act into an act of righteousness. Similarly, testimonies from the

1947 Partition Archive recount phrases like "avenging the dishonor" and "purifying the land," which demonstrate euphemistic and moralized rationales. These statements are consistent with Bandura's notion that violent conduct is made personally and socially acceptable by portraying it as serving socially worthy or moral purposes (Bandura, 1999, p. 194). These accounts reflect how the line between moral and immoral was intentionally blurred. Many perpetrators saw themselves not as violators, but as moral actors correcting perceived wrongs. Survivor accounts from the Partition Archive reinforce this theme, with many recalling that perpetrators justified their actions by referencing the suffering of their community or the divine will. These testimonies are invaluable in showing that violence was not seen as an act of deviance but as a responsibility to uphold or restore honor.

Newspapers and political discourse also played a critical role in legitimizing sexual violence through moral disengagement. *The Statesman* and *Dawn* often published reports that either downplayed sexual violence or contextualized it as part of the broader communal strife. For instance, headlines referring to "reprisals" or "retaliatory attacks" implicitly framed sexual violence as a justified reaction to prior offenses. Press narratives did little to humanize the victims. Instead, they often contributed to a tit-for-tat atmosphere, which served to inflame rather than restrain (Khan, 2007, p. 152). This language facilitated euphemistic labeling, one of the most insidious mechanisms of moral disengagement. These headlines and articles often failed to depict victims with empathy, instead portraying them as collateral damage in a larger communal war. Such representations reduced the psychological weight of committing harm and diffused accountability. Euphemistic labeling in the media normalized cruelty by encoding it in the language of resistance, duty, or revenge. Over time, this constructed a public consensus in which sexual violence was seen as a necessary, even inevitable, consequence of the Partition, legitimizing sexual violence through moral disengagement.

Communal and religious leaders also contributed to the ideological scaffolding that facilitated moral disengagement. Veena Das explains that in some communities, abducted women were referred to as "sacrifices" or "offerings," implying a religious or patriotic nobility to their suffering (Das, 2007, p. 62). In such contexts, perpetrators could see themselves not as criminals but as participants in a moral mission. The blending of violence with spiritual or nationalist discourse created a fertile ground for rationalization and emotional detachment. Dehumanization frequently occurs through moral rhetoric that turns people into problems or threats (Smith, 2011, p. 98). These frameworks stripped victims of individual subjectivity and replaced them with symbolic status as vessels for communal redemption or punishment. Religious and nationalist leaders, through sermons or local directives, often fueled these ideas, embedding them in cultural practices that validated violence. This form of institutional moral disengagement blurred the lines between righteousness and atrocity, framing sexual violence as a sacred or political necessity rather than a criminal act.

This chapter also considers how state inaction contributed to moral disengagement. When local police or administrative authorities failed to intervene—or even participated in violence—this sent a message that sexual violence was tolerated or condoned. The absence of sanction can function as a tacit approval, transforming personal reluctance into active participation (Waller, 2007, p. 101). In many documented cases, survivors recalled appealing to police only to be turned away or ignored. This erosion of legal and moral authority created a vacuum in which perpetrators felt free to act without consequence. The inaction of the state not only removed external deterrents but also affirmed the internal rationalizations of perpetrators. Where law is absent and where institutions remain silent, the burden of guilt is dispersed, and psychological inhibition weakens. Survivors often interpreted this silence as complicity, and for perpetrators, it became yet another mechanism to evade self-reproach. This convergence of institutional failure and moral distortion allowed a widespread culture of impunity to thrive, embedding sexual violence in the sociopolitical transition itself.

The communal narrative of sexual violence as a form of symbolic retaliation further entrenched the moral disengagement of perpetrators. In

Bengal, as Das recounts, stories of women being raped circulated rapidly, generating a communal atmosphere of grievance and justification. These stories did not remain private; they were retold, exaggerated, and ritualized in public discourse, becoming part of the rationale for further violence (Das, 2007, p. 58). In this cyclical logic, one act of violence begets another, and each is seen not as an aberration but as a moral obligation. In this way, sexual violence was not only a tool of harm but also a form of communication—reiterating territorial claims, reinforcing masculine power, and institutionalizing retribution. Over time, such narratives hardened into collective memory, where entire communities internalized the notion that violence was not only justifiable but historically necessary. The normalization of this type of violence through intergenerational storytelling ensured that moral disengagement was preserved and passed down, long after the Partition itself had ended.

Importantly, many perpetrators invoked group membership as a means of diffusing individual responsibility. In interviews collected by the Partition Archive, several witnesses describe scenarios where men justified their actions by saying, "Everyone was doing it," or "I had no choice; the others would have turned on me." This conforms to Bandura's observation that responsibility can be obscured or diffused by dividing labor and attributing decisions to group processes (Bandura, 1999, p. 199). These rationalizations illustrate the psychological insulation that allowed violence to feel normal, even necessary. Moreover, the herd mentality functioned as a psychological shield; as long as actions were performed in concert, the individual moral weight was perceived to be shared and therefore lessened. Peer behavior became the metric for what was permissible. In this context, group dynamics are deeply rooted in human psychology, wherein social belonging often takes precedence over moral evaluation. Silence and complicity can be as powerful as direct incitement. Perpetrators became part of a moral consensus shaped not by laws, but by the approval and expectations of those around them.

Additional evidence from survivor testimonies further highlights the intersection of moral disengagement and communal ideology. One testimony recorded by the 1947 Partition Archive described how a survivor's attacker told her, "This is not about you; it's about your people. You must suffer so they understand." This reflects both dehumanization and the symbolic logic of communal punishment. Here, the victim becomes a proxy for a larger group identity, allowing the perpetrator to rationalize violence as a form of collective justice. The communal dimension of this logic reflects Smith's argument that victims are stripped of individuality and converted into representations of abstract threats (Smith, 2011, p. 145). Such accounts reinforce Bandura's assertion that moral disengagement operates most powerfully when the victim is perceived as interchangeable with a threatening out-group (Bandura, 1999, p. 196). The frequency with which survivors reported hearing similar phrases suggests that these rationalizations were not merely personal but socially conditioned. These testimonies suggest a deliberate, rather than incidental, effort to reframe violence in terms of justice and reciprocity, allowing perpetrators to participate in brutality without self-recrimination. In communities where such reasoning prevailed, perpetrators could see themselves as instruments of divine or communal justice, absolving themselves of personal responsibility.

In *The Pity of Partition (2013)*, Ayesha Jalal discusses how the literary works of Saadat Hasan Manto captured the moral ambiguity and psychological rupture of the time. Manto's stories, such as "Khol Do" and "Thanda Gosht," expose how perpetrators often viewed themselves as victims of history, caught in events beyond their control. Jalal argues Manto's genius lies in his ability to show how perpetrators were also morally disoriented, often clinging to the belief that they were doing what had to be done (Jalal, 2013, p. 167). These narratives highlight how violence could be internalized as inevitability rather than agency. Manto's characters are often fragmented, haunted by their actions yet trapped in a larger moral void. This literary representation aligns with Bandura's theory that moral disengagement can be reinforced through narratives of inevitability, where individuals cease to see alternatives to violence and adopt resignation as moral closure. Manto's characters act not with confidence but with detachment, which is essential in understanding the psychological retreat necessary to perform acts of horror with emotional neutrality. Moreover, Manto's writing offers a critical counterpoint to nationalist and communal discourses, reminding readers that violence often masks itself in the language of righteousness while corroding the human spirit from within.

Religious festivals and rituals were also reinterpreted as opportunities for revenge and purification. In some communities, incidents of sexual violence were timed to coincide with days of religious significance, further entrenching the idea that such acts held a sacred or purgative function. Das highlights the case of a woman abducted on Eid, where her captors told her she was "an offering to God." The religious framing of sexual violence not only distorts spiritual narratives but also provides perpetrators with moral absolution, a dynamic Bandura refers to as the moral restructuring of harmful conduct (Bandura, 1999, p. 197). This phenomenon reflects how ritualistic and symbolic violence gains legitimacy through the invocation of divine or collective ideals. Perpetrators may have felt they were engaging in acts of sacrifice rather than destruction—an inversion that heightens the psychological plausibility of otherwise abhorrent behavior. The implication that rape or forced conversion could carry religious or moral value reveals how thoroughly violence was embedded in the symbolic order of the Partition.

Peer testimony also reveals how younger boys were initiated into violence through observation and coercion. In one case, a witness recalled a group of teenage boys encouraged by elders to "learn to protect their community" by participating in the looting and rape of refugee women (The 1947 Partition Archive, n.d.). This dynamic illustrates what Waller terms "moral apprenticeship," wherein violence becomes a social rite of passage in conflict settings (Waller, 2007, p. 104). Social learning theory supports this interpretation, suggesting that modeling behavior from authority figures creates behavioral norms. Behavior is learned observationally through modeling: from observing others one forms an idea of how new behaviors are performed (Bandura, 1977, p. 22). In the Partition, this modeling was frequently violent, collective, and legitimized by elders—leading to a normalization of brutality among impressionable youth. The internalization of violent behaviors as protective or honorable roles further removed perpetrators from the moral consequences of their actions, allowing violence to be viewed as a contribution to a larger communal mission.

Furthermore, euphemistic language around sexual violence was often adopted by both perpetrators and passive bystanders. Words like "settling scores," "teaching lessons," or "taking what was owed" appear repeatedly in survivor narratives and contemporary accounts. These phrases downplay the brutality of the acts, masking them behind a veneer of justice or necessity. Language that cloaks cruelty makes it easier to commit and harder to confront (Smith, 2011, p. 107). The pervasiveness of such terminology suggests that the normalization of sexual violence was deeply embedded in the Partition's linguistic and social fabric. Euphemistic labeling also reduces cognitive dissonance, allowing individuals to maintain a sense of moral self while committing violence. Thus, language becomes not just a descriptor of action but a tool of psychological transformation. Moreover, when such terminology becomes embedded in political or communal discourse, it reinforces the social acceptability of violence, enabling its repetition across time and geography. Survivors have reported instances where neighbors described the abduction of women as "cleansing the community," revealing how distorted language becomes complicit in violence.

One often-overlooked dimension of moral disengagement is how acts of violence were socially recontextualized through the narratives of perpetrators themselves. In post-Partition interviews and informal recollections, some men who committed sexual violence reframed their experiences not with remorse, but with pride or neutrality. These retrospective justifications—recounted decades later—illustrate that moral disengagement was not only an immediate mechanism during the violence, but an enduring cognitive structure. Self-justificatory mechanisms can persist long after the behavior, shaping one's identity and relationships with others (Bandura, 1999, p. 210). This highlights how moral disengagement embeds itself in collective memory, producing generational silence or glorification around acts that should otherwise invite condemnation. It demonstrates how acts of violence were socially recontextualized through the narratives of perpetrators themselves. In some cases, these men went on to occupy leadership roles within local communities, further entrenching their narratives as historical truth. Their accounts were not just remembered—they were repeated, taught, and absorbed by the next generation, forming a communal mythology in which sexual violence became a tale of heroism or duty rather than atrocity. The absence of critical interrogation of these narratives ensured their longevity, making the moral disengagement self-reinforcing over time.

Another critical facet of moral disengagement during the Partition is the complicity of local institutions and families in facilitating silence. In many instances, families who reclaimed abducted women rejected them, citing dishonor or pollution. This rejection served to affirm the logic of the perpetrators: that these women were now tainted and belonged to the enemy. Das underscores this in *Life and Words (2007)*, observing how "violence is often maintained not only through its performance but through its aftermath—through exclusion, silence, and the failure of reintegration" (Das, 2007, p. 85). This post-violence exclusion created an echo chamber in which the community's failure to restore honor aligned with the perpetrator's original rationale. In doing so, it solidified the cycle of moral disengagement not only among perpetrators, but among victims and bystanders alike. The rejection of victims by their own communities also discourages future testimonies and silences intergenerational dialogue, effectively muting resistance to dominant narratives. In this environment, even acts of survival are framed as shameful, and the psychological burden shifts entirely to the victim. Such social rejection has the dual effect of reinforcing patriarchal values and sustaining communal ideologies that glorify violence as a tool of boundary-making and moral retribution.

Moreover, the reintegration—or lack thereof—of perpetrators into post-Partition society demonstrates how moral disengagement continued long after the violence ended. In many cases, men who had participated in rape and abduction returned to their communities without censure. Some even gained status as "protectors" or "defenders" of the faith. This retrospective moral validation not only reinforces Bandura's claim that people reconstruct their moral agency post hoc, but also underscores the need to interrogate how collective memory sanitizes violence for future political or religious ends. Communities that silence or celebrate past violence create an enduring moral landscape in which similar behaviors may recur. When perpetrators are rewarded instead of punished, they do not see themselves as wrongdoers – they see themselves as heroes (Waller, 2007, p. 108). In this way, the absence of post-conflict accountability functions as both a moral and legal failure. It erases the victim's suffering while reinforcing the legitimacy of the perpetrator's rationale. Survivor silence, whether forced or voluntary, compounds this issue, allowing moral disengagement to calcify into historical truth.

Finally, this uncritical reintegration can shape communal identity in destructive ways. Perpetrators who are lauded as community defenders help cement a dangerous precedent: that violence, especially against marginalized groups, is not only acceptable but admirable when committed under the guise of group protection. The long-term effect of this cultural narrative is the institutionalization of moral disengagement, where future acts of violence are viewed through a lens of justified history rather than ethical reflection. In this way, moral disengagement becomes woven into the community's moral compass, setting the stage for cyclical violence. Without intentional efforts to disrupt these narratives—through education, justice mechanisms, and cultural reckoning—the community remains trapped in a legacy of unaccounted violence that distorts both historical truth and ethical clarity.

CHAPTER 4

PSYCHOLOGICAL & SITUATIONAL MECHANISMS IN ACTION

This chapter applies the theoretical framework of moral disengagement and its allied concepts—dehumanization, diffusion of responsibility, emotional triggers, and situational enablers—directly to acts of sexual violence during the 1947 Partition. While Chapter 3 explored how perpetrators justified their actions through cultural and cognitive rationalizations, this chapter delves into how those justifications translated into violent behaviors in specific environments. It aims to bridge the psychological interiority of moral disengagement with the structural and communal dynamics that enabled mass sexual violence. In doing so, it reinforces the central study: moral disengagement, while necessary, was not sufficient. Instead, it was catalyzed into action through a convergence of psychological manipulation, emotional provocation, and environmental permissiveness.

Moral disengagement found its most visible form in the transformation of everyday individuals into perpetrators under specific situational pressures. Christopher Browning's *Ordinary Men (1992)* demonstrates that "even men who had not previously exhibited violent tendencies became capable of atrocities when embedded in a group setting where violence was normalized" (Browning, 1992, p. 76). This insight is echoed in numerous survivor testimonies from the 1947 Partition Archive. One woman, abducted during a raid on a refugee train in Punjab, recalled that "the men weren't angry; they were silent, methodical like they believed what they were doing was required of them" (The Partition Archive, n.d.). The normalization of such violence, paired with the psychological numbing fostered by repetition, illustrates how moral disengagement becomes behaviorally ingrained through peer conformity and situational enablement.

The influence of emotional catalysts in triggering this violence cannot be overstated. Bandura acknowledges that moral disengagement is often activated by affective arousal—particularly when stoked by fear, rage, or grief—because emotions override cognitive inhibition and accelerate justification (Bandura, 1999, p. 201). In Partition-era India, stories of sexual violence committed by rival communities were frequently exaggerated and circulated to incite vengeance. These narratives of prior harm were not merely reflective but prescriptive—they invited retribution by making it morally compulsory (Das, 2007, p. 59). As groups gathered around makeshift border villages and refugee convoys, such emotional framing created an atmosphere of heightened urgency, where violence felt like justice.

One of the clearest manifestations of situational enablers was the collapse of institutional authority during the months surrounding the Partition. With British colonial forces withdrawing and the Indian and Pakistani states still in embryonic stages of formation, law enforcement was either non-existent or actively complicit in violence. In her research, Yasmin Khan explains that the law had all but vanished in many parts of northern India, and with it, so too disappeared any deterrent against sexual violence (Khan, 2007, p. 138). This vacuum allowed perpetrators to act without fear of legal or social consequences. In effect, the absence of a policing apparatus removed external restraint, while moral disengagement eliminated internal ones.

While emotional triggers and institutional collapse are critical, dehumanization was the psychological linchpin that enabled violence to be sustained. The act of dehumanizing someone is not a precursor to violence—it is the violence (Smith, 2011, p. 144). This was evident in how sexual violence became not just a physical but a symbolic act. Women were targeted not as individuals but as vessels of community honor. In cases documented by Menon and Bhasin, women were paraded naked through towns, forcibly tattooed with religious symbols, and renamed—all acts intended to signify not just personal subjugation, but the subjugation of an entire religious or ethnic group (Menon & Bhasin, 1998, p. 119).

The Role of Peer Pressure and Collective Identity Formation

Peer pressure was not merely a circumstantial influence; it was an active catalyst for the normalization and execution of sexual violence. Stanley Milgram's experiments reveal how individuals defer moral responsibility under perceived authority, but Christopher Browning adds a critical layer by showing how that authority can be diffuse—emanating not from a single leader but from group consensus (Browning, 1992, p. 73). During the Partition, perpetrators were frequently surrounded by friends, neighbors, or fellow refugees whose shared narratives of vengeance, fear, and honor created a moral echo chamber. Survivor accounts confirm that many attackers operated in groups where no single individual led the act, but all shared responsibility. One woman recounted, "There were at least five of them. None said anything. It was like they were all moving on instinct, doing what had already been decided" (The Partition Archive, n.d.). This chilling description reflects how peer settings can diffuse accountability and heighten violence.

Group cohesion also allowed perpetrators to reinterpret their actions as protective or valorous rather than deviant. When violence becomes a rite of group solidarity, dissent is cast as betrayal (Waller, 2007, p. 95). In the context of the Partition, participating in sexual violence was sometimes perceived as defending one's community, particularly when women from the opposing side were portrayed as symbols of territorial or cultural invasion. This process of moral inversion—where cruelty becomes virtue—was bolstered by the ritualistic nature of group violence, turning the act itself into a performance of communal strength. The internal policing within these groups, where silence or hesitation could invite suspicion or ostracism, further eliminated the psychological space for moral reflection or restraint.

Peer dynamics were further reinforced through cultural rituals and gendered expectations that cast participation in violence as a form of masculinity. Violence is not simply the breakdown of social order but the reorganization of it through new rituals of belonging (Das, 2007, p. 70). Young men, especially those coming of age during the Partition, were frequently socialized into acts of violence as demonstrations of maturity, power, and loyalty to their community. This masculine coding of violence placed pressure on individuals to perform brutality as a rite of passage. For many, failing to participate could result in social ostracization, ridicule, or even suspicion of cowardice or betrayal. In this way, peer pressure operated as external coercion and an internalized expectation of identity performance.

These dynamics were particularly pronounced in rural and semi-urban areas where group cohesion was tightly maintained through familial and caste-based affiliations. In such settings, decision-making was often collective, and deviation from group consensus was rare and socially punished. Survivors recount that entire neighborhoods would mobilize together during attacks, with each participant assigned roles—from lookouts to those committing acts of sexual violence—illustrating how deeply the division of violent labor was institutionalized within communal structures. This resonates with Bandura's observation that the diffusion of responsibility in groups weakens moral control by obscuring personal agency (Bandura, 1999, p. 197). In Partition-era India, the group did not merely permit violence—it required it, embedding it within the structure of collective duty.

Moreover, peer-driven participation was often preemptively justified through narratives of victimization and honor, further enabling moral disengagement. Testimonies reveal that attackers would rationalize their actions by referencing stories of similar assaults committed against their own women, even when those stories were based on rumor or exaggeration. Rhetoric and narratives become essential for driving community anger and fear. Whether fictionalized or fact-based, the story becomes a catalyst for a response. This cyclical narrative allowed groups to enter violent encounters already equipped with a moral script. One of the most effective enablers of group violence is the shared conviction that one's actions are defensive rather than aggressive (Waller, 2007, p. 88). Thus, sexual violence became not only permissible but preemptively authorized through the communal logic of defense and restitution.

Ritualization of Sexual Violence and Symbolic Communication

Sexual violence during the Partition also took on ritualistic forms, transforming it from spontaneous acts of brutality into premeditated performances of communal dominance. Lisa Sharlach notes in her work on the Rwandan genocide that rape was not only a method of ethnic cleansing but also a message broadcast to the surviving population (Sharlach, 2000, p. 84). A similar pattern emerged during the Partition. Women were sometimes raped in public spaces, in front of family members, or during religious holidays—each detail a symbolic weapon meant to communicate humiliation, subjugation, and the erasure of identity. These actions were designed to inflict physical pain and broadcast a message: *your community has been conquered.*

This performative aspect of violence elevated it from an individual act to a communal event. David Livingstone Smith's theory that violence against the dehumanized serves as a spectacle as much as punishment (Smith, 2011, p. 122) helps explain why public rape and mutilation were often carried out with an audience. Testimonies from both *The Statesman* and the Partition Archive recount crowds gathering as women were brutalized—sometimes with cheers, sometimes in silence, but rarely with intervention. This passive participation reinforced the communal approval of such acts, embedding them deeper into the fabric of group identity.

The ritualistic nature of violence was also evident in the way sexual crimes were choreographed to reinforce ethnic and religious narratives. Many attacks coincided with significant religious holidays or political events, magnifying their symbolic weight. Rape in the context of ethnic conflict is rarely incidental; it is orchestrated to maximize psychological impact on the community (Sharlach, 2000, p. 83). During the

Partition, rapes conducted during Diwali or Eid were interpreted not merely as violations, but as deliberate profanations of sacred time. This distortion of ritual created a powerful message that no spiritual nor communal space was immune from desecration. It demonstrated to survivors and observers alike that the perpetrators wielded not only physical control but symbolic dominance over every aspect of identity and culture.

Moreover, these violent rituals were not hidden but publicized within the communities that perpetrated them. Menon and Bhasin document cases where abducted women were paraded through streets with banners proclaiming their new religious identity or forced conversions (Menon & Bhasin, 1998, p. 129). These acts were designed to shame the victim and simultaneously celebrate the perpetrator's assertion of power. They also served a dual function: punishing the enemy and signaling moral triumph to one's own group. In this context, rape was not only tolerated but valorized, becoming a form of social capital within tight-knit groups. The collective witnessing of these acts added another layer of ritual—a kind of performative approval that extended beyond the act itself into the broader communal psyche.

The transformation of sexual violence into spectacle also altered the psychological dynamic of bystanders. Spectator violence reinforces shared belief systems by providing public affirmation of those beliefs through collective silence or complicity (Smith, 2011, p. 126). In

Partition-era India, silence was rarely neutral. Crowds that gathered and failed to intervene were participating in a ritual of consent. This collective approval diminished the likelihood of moral reflection or remorse among perpetrators. The community, through its silence or tacit encouragement, helped complete the cycle of moral disengagement, allowing perpetrators to feel both socially affirmed and morally justified.

These performances of ritualized violence also had long-term consequences on intergenerational memory and trauma. Survivors often noted that the theatrical nature of these acts made them unforgettable, with visual and symbolic elements haunting them far more than the physical pain alone. In *Life and Words (2007)*, Veena Das describes how survivors "carry within their bodies the inscriptions of violence—not just through scars but through internalized scripts of humiliation and erasure" (Das, 2007, p. 89). The ritualization of sexual violence, then, ensured that its impact was not only immediate but enduring, woven into the very fabric of memory and identity for those who experienced or witnessed it.

Finally, ritualized violence allowed perpetrators to distance themselves emotionally by framing their actions within structured, even celebratory, social acts. The use of chants, songs, or invocations during assaults, as documented in several testimonies, provided a psychological scaffold that insulated perpetrators from guilt. Structured routines and ceremonial forms provide buffers for ethical disengagement by turning violence into a matter of cultural expression rather than individual accountability (Bandura, 1999, p. 209). These ritualistic forms acted as cognitive scripts, transforming acts of cruelty into accepted—even praised—performances within a group identity. Such rituals did not merely accompany the violence; they justified it, celebrated it, and ensured its replication.

Comparative Perspectives and Reinforcing the Thesis

Understanding the Partition in comparison to other episodes of genocidal sexual violence sharpens the ability to distinguish between context-specific triggers and universally observed mechanisms. In Rwanda, during the Rwandan genocide, as in the Partition, rape was used to violate not only the body but the ethnic essence of the victim. Sharlach describes how "rape was used to destroy the reproductive capacity and the symbolic continuity of the targeted community" (Sharlach, 2000, p. 86). During the Partition, forced pregnancies, conversions, and the renaming of abducted women served a similar function—asserting symbolic dominance by distorting lineage and identity. These parallels strongly support this study's argument that the Partition's sexual violence was not spontaneous but deeply structured by moral disengagement, dehumanization, and group conformity.

Yet, unlike the genocides of Rwanda or Bosnia, where there was some degree of post-conflict recognition and accountability, the sexual violence of the Partition has remained largely unacknowledged in public discourse. This absence of redress has allowed many of the psychological mechanisms explored in this study to remain unchallenged. As Bandura warns, "Without mechanisms of accountability, moral disengagement becomes embedded in the norms of behavior" (Bandura, 1999, p. 215). In South Asia, this silence continues to inform inter-communal dynamics and inhibits the development of empathetic national memory.

In Bosnia, systematic rape camps were used to terrorize and ethnically cleanse Muslim communities, often under the banner of national purity. These actions were not simply opportunistic but were institutionalized as part of a broader political agenda. Scholars like Allen and Seifert have argued that this institutionalization created a bureaucratized form of moral disengagement, where perpetrators saw themselves executing a collective plan rather than committing individual crimes. During the Partition, while there was no central authority orchestrating sexual violence, communal structures like village councils, militia groups, and even refugee caravans replicated similar forms of moral delegation and group cohesion. The mechanisms may have differed in origin, but the psychological outcome—the rationalization of violence through group ideology and symbolic dominance—remained strikingly consistent.

Genocidal rape in the Holocaust context was less visible but still deeply rooted in ideological frameworks. As documented by scholars such as

Dwork and Berenbaum, acts of sexual violence by Nazi forces were rationalized through racial hierarchies that framed Jewish women as impure and dehumanized. This ideological dehumanization mirrors the way Hindu, Muslim, and Sikh communities during the Partition viewed the women of opposing communities—as contaminated, symbolic vessels of threat. The Holocaust teaches that even within highly ordered systems, sexual violence can flourish when moral disengagement is paired with dehumanizing propaganda. The Partition's decentralized chaos did not mitigate these mechanisms—it magnified them by removing formal boundaries and accountability.

What these comparisons underscore is that sexual violence in ethnonational conflicts often transcends individual motivation and reflects systemic narratives of community defense, honor, and purification. In Rwanda, the phrase "cut the tall trees" became a euphemism for genocide, simplifying the act of killing into a communal duty. During the Partition, phrases like "settling scores" and "restoring honor" operated in similar ways, turning unspeakable acts into culturally digestible practices. As Bandura argues, language plays a critical role in facilitating moral disengagement: "People can engage in conduct that is normally restrained by moral concerns by changing how they think about what they are doing" (Bandura, 1999, p. 197). Euphemistic language, therefore, acts as a psychological medium for cruelty, smoothing over ethical resistance.

It is also worth noting how post-conflict narratives diverge dramatically between contexts. In Bosnia and Rwanda, war crimes tribunals and truth commissions have created platforms for acknowledging sexual violence and punishing perpetrators. These judicial processes provide legal justice and help reestablish moral boundaries within societies. In India and Pakistan, no such institutional effort was made to address the Partition's gendered atrocities. This absence has allowed moral disengagement to linger unchallenged in the social fabric, shaping collective memory through silence rather than confrontation. Survivors were not asked to testify but to forget, and in doing so, the broader society forfeited a critical opportunity for moral reckoning.

Furthermore, the intergenerational transmission of trauma differs sharply across these examples. In Rwanda and Bosnia, the public recognition of sexual violence has enabled second-generation survivors to engage in healing practices, even when justice is incomplete. In South Asia, the silencing of the Partition's sexual violence has left its legacy to fester unspoken in families and communities. Children and grandchildren grow up with fragmented stories, whispered warnings, and gaps in familial history. This suppression perpetuates cycles of shame and secrecy, indirectly reinforcing the logic of moral disengagement by treating victims as anomalies rather than as the human consequence of structural violence.

Finally, comparative analysis also illuminates how resistance can be structured against moral disengagement. Survivor testimony in Bosnia and Rwanda has been mobilized for legal proceedings and educational and artistic purposes, restoring voice and dignity to the violated. In South Asia, where such public platforms are limited, the few survivors who have spoken—often through the work of scholars like Butalia, Menon, and Bhasin—have become foundational figures in challenging the moral disengagement that persists. Their voices serve as crucial counterweights to the dominant narratives of honor, sacrifice, and retaliation that have historically justified sexual violence. Through them, it becomes evident that moral disengagement is not absolute—it can be contested, rewritten, and ultimately dismantled.

These comparative insights validate the analytical tools employed in this study and extend their applicability to broader studies of mass violence. They serve as a stark reminder that while the psychological mechanisms may be universal, their expression is always culturally specific. Recognizing this balance between universality and specificity is essential for both understanding past atrocities and preventing future ones. As this chapter has shown, the Partition is not an outlier—it is part of a broader pattern in which moral disengagement, under the right conditions, becomes the engine of extraordinary cruelty.

Addressing Counterarguments

Some scholars argue that Partition-era sexual violence was primarily opportunistic, driven by the chaos of mass migration rather than structured psychological mechanisms. While the lawlessness of the period undoubtedly provided an opportunity, this explanation is insufficient to account for the widespread patterns, symbolic targeting, and consistency of justifications across regions. As demonstrated throughout this chapter, violence was not merely reactive but often planned, endorsed, and ritualized. It functioned within a framework of cognitive rationalizations and emotional mobilizations—both of which point to moral disengagement as a necessary precondition.

Another counterargument is that perpetrators were motivated purely by individual grievance or revenge. This overlooks the evidence of coordinated group actions, public celebrations of violence, and shared rhetoric that framed sexual assault as a communal act. To attribute violence only to individual pathology is to miss its embeddedness in everyday forms of thought and sociality (Das, 2007, p. 65). The mechanisms explored in this chapter—emotional triggers, group conformity, institutional silence, and dehumanization—demonstrate that sexual violence during the Partition was a socially engineered phenomenon, not an accidental byproduct of chaos.

Together, the evidence in this chapter strongly reinforces the argument of this project: moral disengagement is not only a framework for understanding perpetrator psychology but a powerful explanatory tool for how that psychology translates into mass sexual violence under specific situational conditions. Additionally, critics who suggest that moral disengagement fails to account for structural and institutional factors overlook the integrative framework presented in this study. The argument here is not that moral disengagement functions in isolation, but instead that it operates in conjunction with structural breakdowns, group pressure, emotional provocation, and institutional complicity. These dimensions do not compete with psychological mechanisms—they amplify them. In morally disengaged systems, the broader context of complicity sustains individual justifications and removes behavioral constraints (Bandura, 1999, p. 211). The Partition offers a textbook case where the absence of legal authority and the presence of community-sanctioned violence merged to create an environment in which moral disengagement thrived.

A further challenge may come from scholars who argue that focusing on perpetrator psychology risks centering the narrative on perpetrators at the expense of survivors. While this concern is valid, the intention of this study is not to diminish survivor experiences but to understand the cognitive and social mechanisms that made mass sexual violence so prevalent. Without such understanding, prevention efforts remain shallow, focusing solely on punishment or security-based interventions without addressing the underlying belief systems that drive perpetrators. Only by mapping the landscape of perpetrator psychology can one hope to dismantle the architecture of mass atrocity (Waller, 2007, p. 99). Therefore, examining how perpetrators rationalized their actions does not distract from survivor narratives—it helps contextualize and validate them within broader patterns of violence.

Some critics may assert that using post-genocide psychological theory to analyze colonial contexts imposes a framework that is historically or culturally incongruent. However, the psychological mechanisms of moral disengagement, dehumanization, and group conformity are not temporally bound. They have been observed across cultures and centuries—

from the Holocaust to Rwanda, from Cambodia to colonial conquests. What varies is not the existence of these mechanisms but their manifestation in specific cultural contexts. By applying these frameworks to the Partition, this study does not flatten history but enriches it, revealing shared human susceptibilities to violence under conditions of political rupture and communal division.

Lastly, critics might suggest that focusing on sexual violence as a tool of communal violence risks ignoring other forms of Partition-related trauma, such as economic devastation, displacement, and non-sexual killings. This study does not argue that sexual violence was the *only* or even the *primary* form of harm during the Partition. Instead, it identifies sexual violence as a uniquely revealing lens through which to understand how psychological, social, and structural factors converge to produce targeted cruelty. Sexual violence exposes the depth of communal animosities, the symbolic weight of women's bodies, and the readiness of ordinary individuals to engage in morally transgressive acts when provided justification. It is precisely this convergence that renders sexual violence an essential focal point in understanding the psychological mechanisms of mass atrocity.

CHAPTER 5

CONCLUSION – IMPLICATIONS FOR PARTITION AND GENOCIDE STUDIES

This study began with a central question: *how did moral disengagement function as a psychological mechanism in enabling mass sexual violence during the 1947 Partition of India?* Over the course of five chapters, this inquiry has unfolded into a multi-layered examination of how ordinary individuals came to commit extraordinary acts of cruelty, not in isolation, but within a social, emotional, and institutional ecosystem that made such actions not only possible but, in many contexts, valorized. By applying Albert Bandura's theory of moral disengagement alongside allied concepts such as dehumanization, diffusion of responsibility, emotional catalysts, and situational enablers, this book has demonstrated that Partition violence—particularly sexual violence—was not merely opportunistic. It was systematically justified, collectively endorsed, and psychologically insulated from moral scrutiny.

Chapter 1 introduced the theoretical scaffolding necessary to understand how violence becomes morally permissible. Through Bandura's framework and supporting work from Smith, Browning, Waller, Milgram, and Das, the study establishes that moral disengagement is not an abstract or incidental occurrence but a process that can be socially reproduced and sustained. Dehumanization strips victims of empathy. Euphemistic language transforms brutality into justice. Group conformity rewards participation

Fractured Identities | 215

and punishes hesitation. And institutional breakdown removes both external deterrents and moral reference points. Each mechanism on its own may not fully explain the scale of violence, but their intersection creates a perfect storm of moral suspension and collective radicalization.

Chapter 2 applied these theories to the specific regional contexts of Punjab, Bengal, Sindh, and Kashmir. Despite their political, cultural, and demographic differences, these regions showed a disturbing consistency in how sexual violence unfolded. In Punjab, it took the form of mass abductions and ritualized rape. In Bengal, communal rhetoric and media narratives inflamed retaliatory violence. In Sindh, forced conversions were framed as moral or religious victories. And in Kashmir, paramilitary structures enabled systematic assaults under the guise of territorial conquest. These case studies illustrated that moral disengagement was geographically diffuse yet psychologically coherent—it adapted to its surroundings while maintaining a core logic of justification and erasure.

Chapter 3 explored the specific rationalizations perpetrators used to distance themselves from the moral weight of their actions. Testimonies from survivors, press clippings, religious rhetoric, and institutional silence were all examined as mechanisms through which cruelty was reframed as duty. The chapter showed that perpetrators frequently did not view themselves as criminals, but as communal defenders, patriots, or even victims of prior harm. These justifications were not isolated instances; they were socially reinforced through silence, celebration, and the elevation of perpetrators into community heroes. This layer of the study solidified the argument that moral disengagement was not simply reactive but proactive—a tool used to create cohesion among perpetrators and to narrativize violence in retrospect.

Chapter 4 demonstrated how psychological rationalizations translated into violent behavior under specific situational pressures. Emotional catalysts such as grief, rage, and fear were identified as accelerants of moral disengagement, particularly in group settings. Peer pressure, ritualization of violence, and the collapse of legal accountability removed all barriers to action, allowing ideologically justified beliefs to become acts of brutal performance. The chapter also drew comparative insights from genocidal contexts such as Rwanda, Bosnia, and the Holocaust, affirming the global applicability of the mechanisms outlined in this study. At the same time, it emphasized the cultural specificity of the Partition's violence, illustrating how shared human tendencies manifest differently across contexts but often follow similar psychological trajectories.

Together, these chapters support the overarching argument that moral disengagement was a necessary precondition for the mass sexual violence of the Partition, but that it gained traction and lethality only when accompanied by emotional, structural, and social enablers. This convergence transformed individual actors into instruments of communal violence and made acts that would otherwise be morally reprehensible appear acceptable, necessary, or even righteous.

The implications of this study extend beyond Partition studies into the fields of genocide studies, conflict psychology, and postcolonial memory. First, it challenges the notion that sexual violence in communal conflicts is merely a spontaneous byproduct of chaos. Instead, it reframes such violence as structurally embedded, symbolically loaded, and psychologically cultivated. Second, it invites a reevaluation of how societies remember and forget such violence. The lack of public trials, truth commissions, or reparative justice initiatives in the Indian and Pakistani contexts has allowed moral disengagement to persist unchallenged. Survivors were asked to forget, and perpetrators were allowed to rewrite their roles in communal histories. This erasure is itself a form of moral disengagement—a collective decision to prioritize cohesion over truth.

Additionally, this study emphasizes the importance of prevention through cultural, legal, and educational interventions. If moral disengagement can be taught—through language, ritual, and communal narratives—it can also be unlearned. By bringing the Partition's sexual violence into scholarly and public discourse, we not only honor the memory of those who suffered but create tools to recognize and disrupt similar patterns in current and future conflicts. The Partition's legacy is not just a matter of borders and population transfers; it is also a cautionary tale about what happens when communities permit the dehumanization of others in the name of honor, revenge, or survival.

This study also contributes to expanding how to understand perpetrators—not as outliers or aberrations, but as ordinary individuals who became violent under the right confluence of psychological, social, and historical forces. It strategically challenges conventional narratives that frame violence as emerging only from ideological zealots or inherently violent personalities. As Waller explains, "the pathway to atrocity is ordinary," and mass violence is often committed by "those who see themselves as good people doing the right thing under difficult circumstances" (Waller, 2007, p. 45). By studying the mental justifications and social conditions that allowed Partition perpetrators to view themselves as righteous actors, this book opens a crucial avenue for early detection and prevention in modern contexts of rising ethnonationalism and communal polarization.

Moreover, this study provides a framework for analyzing post-Partition silence and denial. While historians and feminists have illuminated aspects of this violence, public commemorations, textbooks, and national discourse often omit or sanitize the brutality, especially the sexual violence. This erasure not only dehumanizes survivors but also protects the psychological mechanisms that enabled violence in the first place. The continued silence around the Partition's sexual violence operates as a collective form of moral disengagement—a refusal to confront the legacy of brutality because it challenges dominant narratives of national pride, martyrdom, and communal righteousness. Recognizing this silence as a form of structural complicity strengthens the case for addressing memory politics alongside justice.

Furthermore, the study emphasizes the importance of integrating moral disengagement theory into peacebuilding and transitional justice initiatives. In conflict resolution settings, interventions often focus on political or economic grievances, overlooking how moral narratives shape the legitimacy of violence. Unless the psychological mechanisms of moral disengagement are dismantled, individuals will find ways to justify violence even in post-conflict conditions (Bandura, 1999, p. 211). In South Asia, where intercommunal tensions remain politically mobilized, these insights could inform curricula, public apologies, or community reconciliation initiatives that address the ideological roots of violence—not just its material effects.

Furthermore, the comparative section of this study reinforced that while the Partition was unique in its geopolitical and colonial contexts, the mechanisms enabling sexual violence are consistent across time and space. From the Holocaust to Rwanda, from Bosnia to Bangladesh, the same toolkit of justification, peer pressure, emotional arousal, and state complicity emerges with haunting regularity. This consistency across contexts validates the applicability of psychological theory to historical inquiry. It also enables scholars to build predictive models for identifying early warning signs of mass atrocity, based not only on troop movements or hate speech, but also on shifts in communal discourse and moral narratives.

Another key takeaway is the role of symbolic violence in transforming acts of sexual aggression into performances of community power. Ritualized rape, public shaming, and forced conversions were not merely tactics of humiliation—they were ceremonies of domination, embedded in political and religious meaning. These performances helped solidify new boundaries between communities, genders, and even generations. Understanding the psychological impact of this performativity helps explain why such violence remains so difficult to discuss, prosecute, or heal from. Survivors carry not only trauma but the weight of symbolic annihilation—an erasure of identity as much as of bodily autonomy.

Furthermore, this book affirms the indispensable role of survivor testimony in challenging the moral disengagement that continues to frame Partition violence. The voices documented by scholars such as Butalia, Menon, and Bhasin offer not only historical evidence but also moral clarity. They refuse to let cruelty be renamed as honor, silence be mistaken for reconciliation, or forgetting to be equated with peace. These testimonies demand recognition not just for their suffering but for their truth-telling, their resilience, and their refusal to be morally erased. In honoring their narratives, this study fulfills its final ethical obligation: to ensure that the psychological machinery that enabled such violence is exposed, interrogated, and ultimately, dismantled.

This book opens the door for future scholarship to examine how moral disengagement and situational enablers operate in other underexplored cases of mass violence in South Asia, such as the 1984 anti-Sikh pogroms, the Gujarat riots of 2002, or the ongoing persecution of marginalized communities. These instances, like the Partition, are shaped by narratives of grievance, communal honor, and retributive justice—fertile ground for moral disengagement to take hold. Scholars could expand the framework used here to analyze how media, state actors, and religious authorities construct the moral legitimacy of violence in these more contemporary cases. Longitudinal studies could also explore how narratives evolve over time and whether communities that have previously participated in or condoned violence develop new moral frameworks in subsequent generations. Such research would not only reinforce the findings of this study but offer a roadmap for addressing the roots of mass violence beyond legal punishment or reconciliation rhetoric.

Equally important is how this study can inform preventative strategies. If moral disengagement is accepted as a socially conditioned process, then it becomes possible to interrupt or reverse it through cultural and educational interventions. Early warning systems that monitor the diffusion of euphemistic language, dehumanizing rhetoric, or ritualized justifications for violence in media and political discourse could help identify when communities are drifting toward collective moral disengagement. Conflict resolution organizations, peace educators, and transitional justice commissions must integrate psychological training that highlights how ordinary people become perpetrators, how justification frameworks take hold, and how to build cognitive resistance to violent groupthink. Prevention, in this sense, becomes not only a political task but a psychological one.

As the study highlights, the role of interdisciplinary research is fundamental in advancing the understanding of mass violence. Historians, psychologists, anthropologists, and legal scholars must collaborate more intentionally to construct nuanced models of how atrocity unfolds. The frameworks applied here are not only relevant to the Partition, but to a host of global contexts where violence is socially produced and morally rationalized. Moving forward, policy design for genocide prevention, post-conflict recovery, and peacebuilding efforts must draw from such interdisciplinary approaches to address not just the outcomes of violence, but the belief systems that justify it. The legacy of the Partition, and the psychological scaffolding that supported its horrors, remains a vital field of inquiry—one that can guide both remembrance and action.

In addition to the theoretical and historical insights, this book contributes to a more robust ethical framework for understanding human rights violations. By focusing on the moral logic of perpetrators, it offers a complementary angle to victim-centered approaches that often dominate transitional justice conversations. This balance is essential; without interrogating how violence is normalized, justice efforts may only scratch the surface. Furthermore, understanding moral disengagement compels societies to evaluate how they foster environments where cruelty can be redefined as community defense or a matter of honor. Institutions, educational systems, and public memorials must actively resist this reframing by promoting narratives that humanize the "other" and honor the complexity of historical truth.

There is also scope to investigate how digital platforms and new media technologies may be modernizing the process of moral disengagement.

As political actors increasingly rely on social media to spread disinformation, euphemistic language, and dehumanizing content, the capacity for moral disengagement has become both accelerated and amplified. In contexts of political unrest or religious polarization, online narratives can rapidly shape public opinion, normalize hate speech, and even incite violence. Scholars and policymakers alike must explore how these modern tools replicate older mechanisms of justification while embedding them in faster, more anonymous systems. A digital-age framework of moral disengagement could provide a necessary expansion of Bandura's original theory, adapted for contemporary threats.

Ultimately, the findings of this study can contribute to an evolving pedagogy on violence prevention. Equipping students, activists, community leaders, and policymakers with language to articulate how moral disengagement works can empower them to dismantle its mechanisms in real-time. Classroom education should include not only the history of events like the Partition but also the psychological patterns that enabled them. Public institutions must adopt restorative justice initiatives that address the social and emotional factors that enable moral transgressions. In sum, dismantling moral disengagement requires more than exposing the lie—it requires building a new moral framework grounded in empathy, accountability, and critical historical reflection.

In this light, the urgency of this book cannot be overstated. The moral stakes of understanding the Partition's sexual violence go beyond academic inquiry—they touch the core of how societies define justice, memory, and accountability. This study is not only a contribution to the intellectual tradition of genocide and trauma studies; it is a moral plea for recognition, truth-telling, and transformation. The women who were raped, abducted, converted, and erased have for too long been exiled from the narrative, treated as collateral damage rather than as central figures in the story of modern South Asia. By bringing their experiences to the forefront, and by dissecting the psychological processes that enabled their suffering, this work honors their truth and insists that society learn from it.

This study insists that violence does not arise from a vacuum, nor does it disappear when the gunfire ceases or when borders are redrawn. It lingers in the stories not told, the names not recovered, the perpetrators not punished. And most dangerously, it lingers in the cognitive blueprints that allow a society to look away, to justify, to forget. The psychological mechanisms explored throughout this study—moral disengagement, dehumanization, euphemism, peer pressure—are not remnants of history; they are active processes in an expanding contemporary world. If society fails to recognize them, it risks repeating the same violence under new banners and in new arenas.

As a result, the premise of this study is not only an act of academic investigation—it is an act of remembrance, of resistance, and of radical empathy. It argues that no study of the Partition can be complete without a reckoning with the cognitive and social conditions that enabled its most intimate cruelties. It affirms that the path to justice must begin with clarity: clarity about what was done, how it was justified, and what must be done to ensure it never happens again. In exposing the psychological infrastructure of sexual violence during the Partition, this work offers not only a mirror to the past but a torch for the future.

Fractured Identities

GLOSSARY

Bosnian Genocide: An ethnic conflict in the 1990s marked by the use of rape camps and forced pregnancies. Its parallels with Partition underscore the global recurrence of gendered violence in ethnic cleansing. (Sharlach, 2000)

Communal Honor: The belief that the dignity of a community rests in its women, often leading to violence against women as acts of vengeance or purification. (Menon & Bhasin, 1998)

Communal Identity: A collective sense of belonging rooted in religion or ethnicity, often invoked to justify violence. During Partition, communal identity became a weaponized framework for defining moral enemies. (Khan, 2007)

Communal Violence: Organized or spontaneous acts of aggression committed by members of one religious, ethnic, or caste-based community against another, often framed as defense of communal identity or retribution. (Khan, 2007; Talbot & Singh, 2009)

Conversion: The forced or coerced change of religion, often through marriage or abduction, used during Partition to symbolically claim ownership over the victim and to erase communal identity. (Menon & Bhasin, 1998; Das, 2007)

Criminogenic Environment: A setting in which the likelihood of committing a crime is increased due to the absence of law enforcement and social deterrents. Partition's lawlessness created criminogenic zones for sexual violence. (Cohen & Felson, 1979)

Dehumanization: The psychological mechanism through which victims are stripped of their human qualities and framed as subhuman, impure, or morally expendable. (Smith, 2011)

Diplomatic Recovery: The post-conflict focus on political normalization rather than individual justice. In the aftermath of Partition, governments prioritized state-building over addressing gendered atrocities. (Menon & Bhasin, 1998)

Diffusion of Responsibility: A mechanism of moral disengagement in which individuals within a group setting feel less personally accountable for collective violence. (Bandura, 1999)

Euphemistic Language: Softened or coded language used to sanitize violence. During Partition, rape was often referred to as "punishment" or "honor restoration." (Bandura, 1999; Das, 2007)

Ethical Judgment: The capacity to discern right from wrong based on moral reasoning. During Partition, ethical judgment was often overridden by collective narratives that redefined atrocity as virtue. (Bandura, 1999)

Gendered Violence: Violence that specifically targets individuals based on their gender. In Partition, gendered violence was used as a means of asserting ethnic and communal control. (Sharlach, 2000; Menon & Bhasin, 1998)

Genocide: The systematic destruction of a religious, ethnic, or cultural group. While Partition is not legally classified as genocide, the patterns of mass sexual violence, displacement, and targeted erasure reflect genocidal intent in localized cases. (Sharlach, 2000)

Group Cohesion: The force that binds members of a group together, often making moral dissent or refusal to participate in violence psychologically costly. (Waller, 2007)

Groupthink: A psychological phenomenon in which group pressure suppresses individual dissent, leading to conformity and moral disengagement. (Milgram, 1974; Browning, 1992)

Identity: The sense of self as shaped by community, religion, and nation. During Partition, violence was used to erase or forcibly rewrite identity. (Das, 2007; Smith, 2011)

Majoritarianism: The dominance of a religious or ethnic majority group, often expressed through systemic marginalization or violence against minorities. (Khan, 2007)

Mob Justice: Acts of violence carried out by groups, often in the absence of formal legal processes, and justified as retributive or protective. (Browning, 1992; Das, 2007)

Moral Disengagement: A process by which individuals cognitively detach from internal moral standards to justify unethical behavior. (Bandura, 1999)

Moral Judgment: The cognitive process through which individuals assess actions as right or wrong. In violent communal contexts, moral judgment can be suspended or distorted to align with group norms. (Bandura, 1999)

Moral Transgression: An act that violates deeply held ethical norms. During Partition, such acts were morally reframed by perpetrators through cognitive mechanisms. (Bandura, 1999)

Partition (The): The division of British India in 1947 into India and Pakistan, marked by mass displacement and sexual violence. (Khan, 2007; Jalal, 2013)

Personalization of Ideology: Internalizing communal or political ideologies as part of one's personal moral code, leading individuals to commit violence with a sense of righteousness. (Waller, 2007)

Perpetrators: Individuals who carried out acts of violence during Partition, often ordinary civilians influenced by peer dynamics and moral disengagement. (Waller, 2007; Browning, 1992)

Political Rhetoric: The use of speeches and discourse to justify or inflame violence. During Partition, political rhetoric helped frame sexual violence as necessary. (Khan, 2007)

Rape: Non-consensual sexual penetration, committed during Partition as a tool of humiliation, symbolic erasure, and ethnic cleansing. (Menon & Bhasin, 1998; Sharlach, 2000)

Religious Polarization: The intensification of religious divisions that legitimizes violence between communities. (Talbot & Singh, 2009)

Rhetoric: Symbolic language used to normalize or glorify violence. Rhetoric during Partition euphemized and legitimized moral disengagement. (Das, 2007)

Routine Activity Theory: Criminological theory stating violence occurs when a motivated offender meets a vulnerable target without protection. (Cohen & Felson, 1979)

Rwandan Genocide: A 1994 genocide in which sexual violence was used systematically. Parallels Partition in its use of rape as symbolic violence. (Sharlach, 2000)

Sexual Violence: Acts of a sexual nature committed during Partition to dominate, erase, and terrorize communities. (Das, 2007; Butalia, 1998)

Situational Enablers: Environmental or institutional factors that create the conditions for violence. (Cohen & Felson, 1979; Khan, 2007)

Statesman, The: A historical newspaper cited for its euphemistic reporting of Partition violence.

Survivors/Victims: Individuals, especially women, who experienced trauma during Partition. Their testimonies provide ethical and historical grounding. (Butalia, 1998; Das, 2007)

Time's Monster (Satia, 2020): A work explaining how historical narratives justify future violence. Useful for framing Partition rhetoric.

Violence: Physical, symbolic, and psychological harm inflicted to assert dominance or erase identity. Often ritualized and morally reframed. (Das, 2007; Smith, 2011)

References:

Bandura, A. (1999). *Moral disengagement: How people do harm and live with themselves.* Worth Publishers.

Browning, C. R. (1992). *Ordinary men: Reserve Police Battalion 101 and the Final Solution in Poland.* HarperCollins.

Butalia, U. (1998). *The other side of silence: Voices from the partition of India.* Duke University Press.

Cohen, L. E., & Felson, M. (1979). Social change and crime rate trends: A routine activity approach. *American Sociological Review, 44*(4), 588–608. https://doi.org/10.2307/2094589

Daily Mail. (1947, March 4). *How India may be split up* [Map]. London: Daily Mail.

Das, V. (2007). *Life and words: Violence and the descent into the ordinary.* University of California Press.

Dawn. (1947–1948). *Dawn Newspaper Archives.*

Government of India. (1949). *The Abducted Persons (Recovery and Restoration) Act, 1949.*

Imperial Gazetteer of India. (1909). *Atlas, Plate 20: Political divisions of the Indian Empire* [Map]. Oxford: Clarendon Press.

Imperial Gazetteer of India. (1909). *Bombay (Northern Section and Sind)* [Map]. In *Atlas*. Oxford: Clarendon Press.

Imperial Gazetteer of India. (1909). *North-West Frontier Province and Kashmir* [Map]. In *Atlas*. Oxford: Clarendon Press.

Jalal, A. (2013). *The pity of Partition: Manto's life, times, and work across the India-Pakistan divide.* Princeton University Press.

Khan, Y. (2007). *The great Partition: The making of India and Pakistan.* Yale University Press.

Menon, K. D. (2012). *Everyday nationalism: Women of the Hindu right in India.* University of Pennsylvania Press.

Menon, R., & Bhasin, K. (1998). *Borders & boundaries: Women in India's partition.* Rutgers University Press.

Milgram, S. (1974). *Obedience to authority: An experimental view.* Harper & Row.

Satia, P. (2020). *Time's monster: How history makes history.* Harvard University Press.

Sharlach, L. (2000). Rape as genocide: Bangladesh, the former Yugoslavia, and Rwanda. *New Political Science, 22*(1), 89–102. https://doi.org/10.1080/07393140008429748

Smith, D. L. (2011). *Less than human: Why we demean, enslave, and exterminate others.* St. Martin's Press.

Survey of India. (1944). *Bengal and Assam and adjacent areas: Distribution of largest communities, 1941 (by smallest available census subdivision)* [Map]. Based on the 1941 Census of India. Government of India.

Survey of Pakistan. (1947). *Map of the United Punjab before Partition showing the notional boundary under the Partition Plan of 3rd June 1947* [Map]. Rawalpindi: Survey of Pakistan Offices.

Talbot, I., & Singh, G. (2009). *The partition of India.* Cambridge University Press.

The 1947 Partition Archive. (n.d.). *The 1947 Partition Archive.* Retrieved from https://www.1947partitionarchive.org/

The Statesman. (1947–1948). *The Statesman Newspaper Archives.*

Waller, J. (2007). *Becoming evil: How ordinary people commit genocide and mass killing* (2nd ed.). Oxford University Press.

About the Author

Krishna A. Patel is a scholar of South Asia and global security, whose work integrates psychology, history, and human rights. He holds a Master of Arts in South Asian Studies from Columbia University and a Master of Science in Terrorism and Homeland Security Policy from American University. His research focuses on the intersections of political violence, collective memory, and the psychology of atrocity in transitional societies.

Patel's scholarship explores diverse topics, including postcolonial state violence, international humanitarian law, and the psychology of genocide. His work includes extensive in-field research on international human trafficking.

Professionally, Patel has held roles in government affairs, cybersecurity, and security policy analysis, advising on global regulatory compliance, crisis management, and foreign policy. His expertise has been applied in both public and private industries, from aerospace applications to governmental institutions.

Patel's scholarship reflects a personal and academic commitment to understanding South Asia's past, as well as that of other transitional societies. He seeks not only to analyze history but to engage with its ethical imperatives: honor survivors, challenge silences, and offer frameworks to prevent the recurrence of mass violence.

www.ingramcontent.com/pod-product-compliance
Lightning Source LLC
Chambersburg PA
CBHW050858160426
43194CB00011B/2209